BLAZE
CLIMBER

THE LATTICE GARDENER

WILLIAM C. MULLIGAN

Foreword by Rosemary Verey

MACMILLAN · USA

Copyright ©1995 by William C. Mulligan

Photography ©1995 by William C. Mulligan and Elvin McDonald
(Others noted on page 188)

MACMILLAN
A Simon & Schuster Macmillan Company
1633 Broadway
New York, NY 10019-6785

MACMILLAN is a registered trademark of Macmillan, Inc.

Library of Congress Cataloging-in-Publication Data

Mulligan, William C., 1942–1995
        The lattice gardener / William C. Mulligan ;
           p.   cm.
        Includes bibliographical references.
        ISBN 0-02-587885-9 (HC)
        1. Trellises.   2. Ornamental climbing plants.
        3. Gardening.   I. McDonald, Elvin.   II. Title.
        SB473.5.M84   1995
        717   dc20   95-8158
                   CIP

Captions for display photographs that appear throughout this book can
be found on page 188.

Printed in the United States

10 9 8 7 6 5 4 3 2 1

In memory of my late father,
William Charles Mulligan II,
a structural engineer of impeccable integrity
and a man of far-reaching generosity
AND
the late Kenneth Charles Neumeyer,
a fellow lattice buff who was ever on the
lookout in my behalf.

CONTENTS

But spite of Heaven's fell rage,

Some beauty peep'd

through lattice of sear'd age.

SHAKESPEARE
A Lover's Complaint

**FOREWORD
BY
ROSEMARY
VEREY**

When William Mulligan asked me to contribute a foreword to his book The Lattice Gardener, *I was delighted. His father was a structural engineer and my husband, David, is an architectural historian, so it seemed to me naturally appropriate. We are kindred spirits in the garden, and Bill knows my appreciation of the use of structural and architectural features.*

After your house, the walls, gates, fences, pergolas, gazebos, and arbors, and all the other elements that make up the architecture of a garden are eye-catching features, striking in their own right as well as providing shelter, shade, and a skeletal framework for climbing plants. I first fully realized the importance of height in the garden, especially on flat terrain, when we were laying out our ornamental potager *twenty years ago. We introduced standard roses and clipped bushes, an apple tunnel and two bowers for seats. I am pleased that this is illustrated in William's book.*

This book is both scholarly and practical, written by a designer who has listened to his woodmen, worked with his carpenters, and learned from them how to achieve his elegant treillage. Talent, imagination, and, perhaps most important, an emphasis on the quality of workmanship go hand-in-hand. It is all too easy to buy ready-made trellis these days at garden centers. More demanding—and much more rewarding—is to personalize these and design your own. But this is not a joinery manual. Here history, artistry, and carpentry are all explored— nor is horticulture neglected, for there is a mouth-watering list of climbers that will happily clamber over your architectural creations.

For nine years William Mulligan has been gathering together material worldwide as an inspiration for gardeners everywhere. This labor of love is his lasting reward.

Rosemary Verey

April 1995

PREFACE

Inspiration has a way of finding its mark in the most unusual and unforeseen ways. In 1987, gardening authorities C. Z. Guest and Elvin McDonald were planning an exhibit for the Horticultural Society of New York's annual flower show to showcase C.Z.'s celebrated greenhouse collection. In a quandary, they needed some kind of staging to flatter the exhibit's temperamental stars: masses of ethereal orchids mostly, but also vining abutilon, azalea topiaries, and amaryllises. They did not know where to turn.

Somewhere from the lower echelons of C.Z.'s imperial court at Old Westbury on Long Island's North Shore, a humble voice piped up, "I can do that." I know not where it came from, but inspiration as sure as a divine calling struck me at that moment. I immediately envisioned a lattice fantasy, with a gazebo (provided prefabricated by Vixen Hill Gazebos) as its centerpiece, to accommodate the space chosen from the show's floor plan. I had never done anything like this before (although I had

absorbed more than I had known over the shoulder of my late father, a structural engineer and highly skilled draftsman, and I was amazed by my temerity.

That moment marked the beginning of an enchanting personal odyssey that has continued unabated to the present. And this book is a coming together of all of the photography and designs accomplished during this wondrous journey.

Where does inspiration come from and why am I so unabashedly passionate about the medium of latticework? No one can answer these questions with certainty, but I sometimes fantasize that my thrall is a holdover from a previous life. Perhaps I was one of Louis's minions at Versailles, who toiled feverishly to satisfy the king's insatiable appetite for structural fantasy, or—dare I be so presumptuous?—perhaps I was treillage designer extraordinaire, Daniel Marot (1663–1752) himself.

One thing I know for sure is that my love of lattice is inborn, something that comes from the heart. The medium itself is spiritual in essence. Not only has it been a part of man's existence since the dawn of history, it seems to be something intrinsic in all of us. Neurophysiologists suggest that the grid pattern, or criss-crossing matrix, is encoded into our DNA, an indelible part of the mind's eye that is as inescapably familiar as a web to a spider or a honeycomb to a bee.

The key word in all of this is love, *the power that fires the universe. To those of you who share my passion, I offer a survey of everything you need to know to fulfill your own unique expressions of the medium. Love can accomplish all things, and with a keen appreciation of the infinite splendor of plants and flowers, you will know instinctively how best to lend them support and crown their glory with architecture.*

I dedicate this book to those incurable romantics who have empathized with my devotion to latticework in all its delightful expressions and to the vining plants that joyfully clamber over their structures.

The Legacy of Our Forebears

Sun-dappled shadows. The luxuriant fragrance of a rose. A kiss stolen in the secret embrace of a bower of intoxicating jasmine. A peekaboo tease through lattice apertures. Intrepid vine tendrils searching blindly for their next moorings. Confidences shared under the comforting shelter of a gazebo. A moment of rest from planting or pruning. A sigh of contentment prompted by the beauty of one's garden. Delicate fretwork. Reassuring posts. Scene-framing windows. Doorways that beckon bewitchingly and arches that vault the awesome grandeur of Nature's handiwork.

Such are the joys and rewards of garden architecture. Its inherent romance is its most inspiring and sustaining aspect, one that has escaped the notice of scarcely a single civilization since the beginning of recorded time. Open, airy structures that bridge the transition between indoors and out have always served as the gathering places and focal points of mankind's gardens. Trellises, arbors, pergolas, gazebos, summer houses, kiosks, temples-of-love, pavilions, Chinese pagodas and *t'ings*, Japanese tea houses, fanciful shelters of some form or other have

The grand lattice pavilions at Old Westbury Gardens provide
endless inspiration. Built in 1906 for John Shaffer Phipps's aristocratic
young English bride, designed by English architect
George Crawley, and preserved to perfection to this day, their spell casts
a timeless chinoiserie splendor over the entire Italian Walled Garden.

stood the test of time like stalwart sentinels on all of history's landscapes, from ancient Egyptian, Greek, Roman, and Asian, to medieval European and Colonial and Victorian American.

My own designs are a sanguine celebration of these antecedents. Most especially, I am drawn to the decidedly formal attitude of the wonders of seventeenth and eighteenth century France. Who can resist the elaborate tributes to Louis Quatorze at Versailles and others among the confections of the unerringly stylish French? The aristocratic majesty of these structures, their gratifying symmetry, speak to me with the utmost eloquence.

I have never in any way copied these examples. My designs are, for the most part, original, informed by their sites and functions and adapted to the architecture of the houses they embellish. But my work owes much to its ancestors, especially to the Victorians and Edwardians, as well as the French. I have also gleaned an abundance of riches from the sublime aesthetics of the designs of Thomas Jefferson and this century's Sir Edwin Lutyens and Ogden Codman. This in no way suggests that I have not found delight in every attempt through the

ages, or that I have not learned something from each.

Of the two basic approaches to all garden design, formal and naturalistic, formal is by far the older, and the more dependent upon architecture and ornamentation. Its roots, predating history, can be traced to the cradles of civilization, the fertile banks of the Tigris, Euphrates, and Nile Rivers. As early as 3000 B.C., elaborate gardens incorporating terracing and water elements had already been laid out by the enterprising Sumerians and Egyptians.

The spoils of war throughout history have frequently yielded much more than territory and destruction. The mighty Persian Empire, with its conquest of Egypt and Assyria in the sixth century B.C., acquired the tastes of its captives, resulting in impressive gardening accomplishments that, in turn, inspired the Moslems who vanquished the Persians. Like unseen underground suckers, the seminal garden fashions of Sumeria spread to Greece and Rome and, ultimately, to all the nations of Europe. The Mongols took them to India, and the Conquistadors of Spain, after invasion by the Moors, carried them to the Americas.

For rose aficionados, the Cranford
Rose Garden in the Brooklyn
Botanic Garden in full bloom is one of
the most spectacular displays to be
seen. Equally impressive is the
magnificent Rose Pavilion, a lattice
odyssey completely entrenched in
climbing roses, which fronts a long
expanse of rose borders.

Devoted Partnerships

Landscape architects and garden designers often refer to the "bones" of the garden when describing the structural outlines and underpinnings that form the foundation for its flowers, shrubs, trees, and vines. Not unlike what a frame does for a painting, these architectural features work to enhance the plantings and showcase their best features. Very few gardens succeed without the support of their skeletons.

In the history of garden design, there have been a number of male-female partnerships that reflect this duality of bones versus plants and flowers. Three that are especially noteworthy flourished in the early part of this century. In each, the woman presided over the plants and flowers, while the man wrestled with the architecture. I am convinced that this gender-specific pattern is merely an accident of history. There is no reason to believe that the roles could not just as well have been reversed. The operative word here is devotion, each partner to the other and both to the perfection of the gardens on which they collaborated.

To begin with, there was the endlessly fascinating Vita Sackville-West

ABOVE, *Sometimes the simplest of materials renders the noblest of effects. At Sissinghurst Castle, Vita Sackville-West and Harold Nicolson appropriated some old stone and wood fragments to create a comfortable sitting area—one with an Old World ambiance. The wisteria clinging to the wall and just beginning to bloom adds to the total effect.*

RIGHT, *A bench, not unlike the classic lyre-back designs of Edwin Lutyens, is set snugly in a living niche with an opening pruned to reveal the view beyond. It is one of Hidcote Manor Garden's many hidden delights.*

and her husband, Harold Nicolson. To the gratitude of a coterie of inveterate gardeners who are familiar with her inspiring words, Vita left the world with a prolific outpouring of writing that chronicles her planting efforts and reflects her philosophical musings and observations.

As a woman, Vita was excluded from the line of inheritance of her family manse, Knole, so in 1930, she purchased Sissinghurst. In the ensuing years, she and Harold transformed the derelict Elizabethan castle into a garden paradise.

As a Member of Parliament, a cabinet minister to Sir Winston Churchill, and a renowned diarist, Harold more than held his own against the considerable accomplishments of his wife. But it was the pair's enduring devotion to each other and the love they lavished on their fabled garden that has given the world a priceless legacy. Their progeny lives today, and any gardener visiting the Cotswolds in southern England would sooner eat dirt than miss a visit to Sissinghurst.

Contributing enormously to the reconciliation of architecture and plants was the famous English duo, Gertrude Jekyll and Sir Edwin Lutyens. Miss Jekyll was trained as an artist, but failing eyesight in later years shifted her attention to garden design and writing. Bringing her unerring eye to bear on the design of the border and its mixes of color, she raised the bounteous English perennial garden to the standard against which all examples since have been measured.

Edwin Lutyens supplied the architectural restraint that allowed Miss Jekyll the freedom to plant with abandon and overflowing abundance. His balustrades, walls, and terraces were the perfect foil for her exuberant plantings. He is probably best known in this country, however, for a single piece of garden furniture. His slatted, lyreback bench is an attractively welcome feature in any garden. Whether enamelled, stained, or of weathered teak, this classic piece, a familiar sight in our nation's gardens as well as in those of England, always adds an elegant focal point.

The Americans Edith Wharton and Ogden Codman blended their talents to produce extraordinarily original interiors that borrowed from the magnificence of the past. Among their accomplishments in the first decades of this century were the upper floors of Cornelius Vanderbilt's The Breakers, one of the many staggeringly opulent mansions and gardens open to the public in Newport, Rhode Island. The two collaborated on a book, *The Decoration of Houses*, that remains to this day one of the bibles of American interior designers.

But Miss Wharton was also an outstanding garden designer who contributed much to a distinctly American style. And her cohort, Ogden Codman, was an inveterate lattice fancier and one of my great-

est sources of inspiration. His highly significant contribution deserves special consideration, and I will devote more attention to him later, in my discussion of treillage in America (see pages 70–71).

Garden structures through the ages encompass a plethora of sizes, shapes, materials, and styles. While some defy classification, most fit loosely into the following categories.

THE TEMPLE OF LOVE

With a name befitting its romantic history, this structure enjoyed its germination in classical Greece and its full flowering in ancient Rome. Contemplating its classic form, one can almost see Dido and Aeneas being teased by Cupid in the embrace of its protective columns. Almost always of stone, these supports were customarily topped with a domed roof of solid stone or copper but sometimes with the airiness of metal filigree.

In ancient times, these temples were often inhabited by a statue of some mythological deity. Today, they are prized for the elegant ornamental focus they bring to the landscape and the strength of support they ensure for heavy-growth vines.

While many of the extant examples of the temple of love, found mostly in public botanical and estate gardens, are much too grand for the confines of today's average garden, this is a versatile structure. It can easily be scaled down in size and made of lighter materials.

Revived in miniature, this gracious monument can be made to accommodate limited spaces without losing any of its noble proportions or classic appeal.

LEFT TOP, *A temple of love with a metal filigree dome supported by stone columns lends a stately focal point on the shores of a pond at Old Westbury Gardens.*

LEFT CENTER, *The park setting embracing the celebrated Columbus, Ohio, rose garden would surely be the lesser without this striking metal temple and gathering place.*

LEFT BOTTOM, *A classic temple at Huntington Botanical Gardens in California might just as well be in ancient Rome.*

RIGHT, *This magnificent temple glints in the sun as it presides at the top of a hill in the Queen's Garden at the Royal Botanical Gardens at Kew.*

I frequently rely on this Greco-Roman innovation in my own work simply because it has the sturdiness required for the woody trunks of a vine such as a wisteria, to say nothing of its timeless beauty. The name comes from the Latin *pergula*, meaning extension, because this structure, spanned at the top by heavy wooden beams, began life as an adjunct to a house or temple, to which one end was attached while the other was held up by a row of columns. Modern interpretations have taken advantage of this feature, providing a most attractive way to shelter a terrace or driveway adjacent to the house.

ABOVE, A pergola with a difference—its roof peaks rebelliously at the center—is the creation of Houston architect R. Michael Lee.

BELOW, A classic painted pergola shelters a silvery weathered teak bench in the Dunn Rose Garden at the Birmingham Botanic Garden.

As time marched on, the pergola moved away from clinging to edifice walls and became a free-standing colonnade. In this incarnation, it reached its ultimate versatility. In modern-day usage, it can provide a home for vines of all kinds, while at the same time forming a graceful, protective covering over a walkway or bench or alongside a pool or tennis court. Depending on the amount of plant support or protective shade required, the beams at the top can be closely or widely spaced.

One of the nicest features of a pergola is that it can be overlaid with a layer of tightly spaced narrow slats across the heavy beams already in place. These will provide increased shade, plus moorings for creeping fine-growth vines. Clear or smoked Plexiglas sheeting across the top of the structure will allow

LEFT, *The same pergola designed by R. Michael Lee (see top photograph on opposite page) becomes a glorious celebration of grape vines in summer.*

RIGHT TOP, *A sitting area under a pergola thwarts Seattle's endless rains with a Plexiglas covering.*

RIGHT BOTTOM, *There is no reason why pergolas cannot be built on a curve. This appealing public walkway in southern California is covered with garlands of bougainvillea.*

you to snuggle into its confines and stay dry despite the heaviest of summer showers. The application of lattice panels between the columns not only allows extra footing for upwardly mobile roses and other vines of a delicate nature, but it also lends privacy from prying eyes and shelter from wind and sun.

THE GAZEBO

The gazebo as we know it today probably began in Holland, tucked into the corners of gardens and along the banks of the canals. Its earliest manifestations were round, sometimes square, structures that were, for the most part, enclosed. Almost always of brick or stone, with peaked thatch or cedar roofs, these charming little buildings were used for the storage of garden tools and equipment, root crops, or dried plant materials.

The word, incidentally, according to *Webster's*, is most probably a marrying of the English "gaze" with the Latin suffix "ebo," yielding the centuries-old coinage, "I shall gaze." As a description of a restful viewing pavilion, the moniker could not be more apt.

As Europe dealt with its wars and conflicts and approached modern maturity, the gazebo began losing its sides. Liberated from blind enclosure, it became a vantage point for viewing the garden, a shelter for repasts and libations and the romantic trysting place of lore. The idea swept westward in the colonization of America, and the kinds that made their way to these shores may be seen today in Colonial

LEFT TOP, *Structures much like this one at Hidcote Manor Gardens in Gloucestershire, England, were the forerunners of today's gazebos.*

LEFT UPPER MIDDLE, *Lacy metal filigree was the order of the day when this gazebo, overlooking the Mississippi River, was built at Rosalie in Natchez, Mississippi.*

LEFT LOWER MIDDLE, *The tightly spaced lattice of this impeccably proportioned pavilion at Rosedown Plantation, St. Francisville, Louisiana, provides an illusion of privacy.*

LEFT BOTTOM, *An enclosed structure at Sissinghurst Castle in Kent, England, proves that a service building need not be unattractive. In the distance are fields of rape, blooming in phosphorescent yellow.*

Williamsburg. One example there that I find especially noteworthy sports Chinese Chippendale–design railings that are as in vogue today as they were in the eighteenth century.

The gazebo reached its ultimate expression in this country in the nineteenth century. The Victorians favored two extremes in design. On the one hand, they pioneered the rustic look, which was a celebration of Nature's handiwork unadulterated. Raw boughs and twigs, inventively positioned to form gazebolike structures, were especially complementary to forested settings and plantings of native species and wildflowers. A wonderful collection of these structures, all overlooking spectacular views of the Adirondack Mountains, can be found at The Mohonk Mountain House, a resort in New Paltz, New York.

On the other hand, under the sway of Gothic, Swiss, and German influences, the Victorians pushed the gazebo to new levels of froufrou and fussiness, not unlike the busyness they favored in their paisley planting beds. No excess was too much, and wherever it could be squeezed in, gingerbread was the order of the day. The industrious Victorians were also responsible for

ABOVE, *Armsful of crape myrtle embrace a wonderfully proportioned pavilion designed by Judy Cloninger of Galveston. One of its most endearing features is a cushioned swing within the pavilion.*

inflating the gazebo to larger proportions and turning it into the park bandstand, the *sine qua non* of community centerpieces.

The gazebo has as much, if not even greater, versatility as the temple of love and the pergola. Its sides can range in number from four to eight, with at least one section left open for entry and exit. A constant feature of the gazebo is a handrailing defining the perimeter's closed sides, but the adaptability of this structure lends itself to interchangeable panels. Fitted with tightly configured lattice, for example, and with a roof of evenly spaced slats, it becomes a shade house for growing certain sun-shy exotics such as orchids. Installed with glass windows, it turns into a greenhouse sanctuary against winter's freezes. With the installation of wire screening insets, both people and plants avoid the nuisance of mosquitoes and other bothersome insects.

A mischievous cherub stands guard before a gazebo of handsome pastel hues. A Chinese Chippendale railing complements the structure's Jeffersonian roots.

THE T'ING

The Far East's equivalent to the gazebo and the pergola is the *t'ing*. Inviting comparisons with both structures, this unique shelter bears the unmistakable stamp of the Orient. Its romantic mystique, nourished with bright colors and rococo filigree, recalls visions of Shanghai and Hong Kong, Asian lanterns, and ancient Chinese landscape paintings.

Descended from a completely enclosed garden house with latticework windows and doors, the *t'ing* in time opened itself to the landscape. The structure is usually square or rectangular and fitted with a wall at its back. A grillwork window or two set into this backdrop is a common variation. The remaining three sides are ordinarily left open, with the occasional addition of a low stone balustrade, akin to a gazebo's railing.

A bold embellishment of the garden, as well as a place for enjoying it restfully, this enchanting edifice is distinguished by a gracefully bowed roofline composed of overlapping clay tiles. Each of its distinctive upward-sweeping corners is normally supported by unadorned stone or wooden pillars.

At the New York Flower Show in 1989, for which I designed an exhibit, I was given the rare privilege of observing close-hand the step-by-step assembly of an authentic *t'ing*. It was the first time the People's Republic of China had participated in an exhibition of this kind in the United States, and they had shipped directly to the site of the show on the floor of enclosed Pier 92 on the Hudson River, four or five huge wooden crates accompanied by a team of workers.

The crates were disassembled with ease, revealing granite slabs that were at least one foot by ten feet by four feet in size. These were positioned to form the floor of the *t'ing* by two small but powerful men who levitated each of the stones. The miracle was accomplished with the help of a thick bamboo pole borne between the men, each end on one man's shoulder. Ropes that had already been positioned under the granite in the crates were drawn up and tied to the pole ends. The men lifted the stones using the power of their legs. Like two Davids slaying Goliath, they drew upon age-old resourcefulness to extend their strength far beyond what would seem humanly possible.

In the days that followed, work

on the *t'ing* concentrated on the assembly of its roof. The tireless laborers painstakingly placed clay tiles, one by one, in overlapping rows. This operation went on for so long that its completion in time for

the opening was cast in doubt. But to everyone's delight, it was completed just under the wire. The *t'ing* proved to be one of the show's greatest crowd pleasers, and at the end of its successful New York run, it was spared a return voyage across the seas; an anonymous benefactor purchased it, lock, stock and barrel, and it now rests on these shores, radiantly crowning an American garden.

A Chinese t'ing is the Eastern expression of the Western gazebo. This one, photographed at the 1989 New York Flower Show, was shipped in thousands of pieces from China.

THE PAVILION

Pavilion seems to be the catch-all word for every garden haven that does not fit comfortably into any of the previous categories. The word was born of the Latin *papilio*, meaning butterfly and also tent, whose canvas flaps evoke images of the insect's wings. Indeed, the knights of the Great Crusades were so taken with the commodious, elaborately fitted canopies they encountered in the deserts of the East that they brought the idea back to Europe as the progenitor of more substantial pavilions to come.

This is not to say that tents in their original form did not survive the ages to become distinctly interesting elements on the contemporary landscape. Relatives of the canvas beach cabana, these mostly round, draped shelters of colorful, frequently striped cloth and pointed roofs make appealingly whimsical statements in many of today's gardens, especially those of tropical regions and otherwise sultry climes.

One year at the Chelsea Flower Show in London, I found an assortment of tents of this kind displayed for sale. Some flew brightly colored banners, adding an infectious festivity to the event, and all promised cool, absolutely shaded refuge from the sun's searing rays.

The eighteenth century French dubbed *pavilions* those rather substantial, yet comparatively small, satellite buildings of the great chateaux that members of the court could escape to for privacy. Though constructed of stone and ornately embellished, these little jewels encompassed no more than one or two rooms and were fitted generously with windows onto the gardens. The most well-known example is the Petit Trianon, Marie Antoinette's hideaway at Versailles. Restored to its original splendor in recent years, its perfection now awaits the admiration of visitors.

It was not until the nineteenth century that the word *pavilion* broadened its horizons to become the concept as we know it today: an open-sided but covered shelter of some kind, a tent at a circus or bazaar, an ample, protected resting place in a community park. Among my own designs, those that I find myself naming pavilions tend to be shaded alcoves larger than a gazebo, at least partially of lattice, that look onto, hugging cheek-by-jowl, features of the landscape reserved for recreation, such as swimming pools and tennis courts.

TOP LEFT, *The parterre beds and tree-form standard roses of this garden are crowned by an elegant pavilion in naturally aged wood. It was designed by Houston's Ed Eubanks.*

TOP RIGHT, *A spanking new curving lattice pavilion on the grounds of Gene and Georgia Mosier in Sewickley, Pennsylvania, will be the site of many happy gatherings.*

BOTTOM LEFT, *The simplicity of this lattice pavilion at Rosalie in Natchez, Mississippi, is its greatest asset. While adorning the landscape unobtrusively, it provides cool shade for garden strollers.*

BOTTOM RIGHT, *This 20'x20'x20' pavilion was designed to provide shade and shelter for poolside frolickers.*

ABOVE LEFT, *Metal is a viable, yet expensive, material for lattice.*
Its greatest advantage is its durability. This splendidly ornate
pavilion resides in Houston's River Oaks neighborhood.

ABOVE RIGHT, *The Staitey House is situated in Sam Houston Park, where it and many others of Houston's grand old houses have been gathered for preservation and appreciation. Some of the lattice of this impressive manse was partially restored and added to at the time of the move.*

THE ARBOR

An old chestnut among gardeners holds that the only things you cannot take with you through a garden arbor archway are your cares and woes. As the garden's time-tunnel passageway to peace and tranquillity, this beckoning walkthrough demands that all worldly strife be left behind.

But what exactly is an arbor? The word is used to describe a number of structural forms whose *raison d'être* is to support climbing and vining plants. The grapevine was probably history's seminal climber in this respect, and there is evidence in tomb paintings that the

ABOVE, *A terrace garden surrounding a nineteenth-floor penthouse is thriving horticulturally—a near miracle. The most impressive feature is two lattice archways crossing each other. Architects refer to this conjoining as a "groined arch." The penthouse garden was the residence of designer John Burgee, of the celebrated architectural partnership Philip Johnson & John Burgee, and was a collaboration between John Burgee and Tim Duval (see pages 76 and 77).*

ABOVE, *Arbors over gateways is a winsome partnership. In summer, the arbor over the entrance to the children's garden at the Brooklyn Botanic Garden is heavy with climbing roses.*

BELOW, *In winter, bereft of roses, the same arbor's form is bared in a field of winter snow.*

arbor was not unknown to the ancient Egyptians. Some of what are called arbors today approach the size and scope of pavilions and pergolas. But I personally attach the word specifically to a simple metal or latticed-wood arch, one that may be easily trotted about the garden to vault a path, a bench, a gate, or such ornamental elements as fountains and statuary.

BELOW, *An arbor entirely covered with English ivy at Jasmine Hill, a formerly private garden near Montgomery, Alabama, is now available*

When the arch is extended along a walkway, it turns into an inviting tunnel, referred to in architectural jargon as a gallery. As far back as the Middle Ages, the French had a selection of names for these enticing coverings, the most obvious among them, *tunelles*. The experience of negotiating a tunnelway and emerging into the sunlight is one of the lattice garden's great pleasures.

for viewing by the public. The ivy arch invites strollers to go up the steps and beyond to discover a ruined garden with a reflecting pool, classic columns, and other stone remnants.

LEFT, *Tubular metal is among the myriad materials that may be used to lift and support vining plants. This artistic example, in copper tubing, was designed by John Yang for a private town house garden in Manhattan.*

THE FENCE

It was the eminent American poet Robert Frost who wisely suggested that good fences make good neighbors. Indeed, a good fence has held a revered position in human territory since the dawn of civilization. Nothing in the vast inventory of mankind's architecture comes close to satisfying so many needs and serving so many functions simultaneously.

Among the many roles fences take on with uncompromising dependability are: demarcation of property lines, management of animal herds, security against intruders, protection from wind and sun, shielding from prying eyes, and support for vining and climbing plants. But the supreme utilitarian nature of the fence need not preclude its ornamental value. While an ascetic, stockade-style plank fence may do the job with dependable efficiency, it does little to enhance the beauty of flowers and plants. There simply is no reason why a fence, whether a barrier, a frame for a border, or a support for vines, cannot be aesthetically pleasing, while fulfilling practical demands.

Whether executed in metal or wood, the design of a fence is an

ABOVE, *This appealing herb garden in Huntsville, Alabama, is enclosed by a simple picket fence.*

An inviting gateway graciously interrupts a handcrafted lattice fence in a private garden in Birmingham, Alabama.

LEFT TOP, *The Lattice Garden at Butchart Gardens in Victoria, British Columbia, can be counted upon to be a riot of color in summer. The great masses of pink geraniums, as seen in the background, grow from troughs resting along the top of the lattice fence.*

ABOVE, *Wattling is as ancient as the British civilization. The technique involves the weaving of young, pliable twigs and boughs—often of willow— and therein lies its sturdiness. Its basketlike demeanor is the perfect complement for many kinds of plantings.*

LEFT BOTTOM, *This handsome and very old lattice fence lines the northern end of the Cranford Rose Garden at the Brooklyn Botanic Garden.*

opportunity for the imagination to take flight. For the 1988 New York Flower Show, I was assigned floor space that ran down the center of the pier and measured eight feet wide by forty feet long. The only possible solution for this impossible geometry was a fence, one that would be viewed by crowds on both sides. But this would be no ordinary fence. Using elements from the previous year's show and adding more, I created a wooden lattice fantasy that was like a story unfolding as one meandered along its length. Breaking out of the flat, two-dimensional plane, this fence incorporated mini arbors, finial-topped poles, latticed columns, shelves supporting container plants, and a grandly arched gateway centerpiece. These elements worked together to lend relief to the otherwise featureless surface, catapulting the idea of a fence to rarefied heights.

Gardeners and nongardeners alike have been experimenting with fence design for centuries. From the tightly tied bamboo canes of the ancient Japanese to the rustic basket-weave wattles of the British Isles, the fence has always respected the styles of the people whose needs it meets. Also, the fence is frequently a good starting point, especially when latticework is the major assembly component in the design of any garden structure. By arranging fence sections, or prefabricated lattice panels available at lumber yards and home improvement centers, in various configurations, an array of free-standing units can be achieved. Their amazing variety will be limited only by the imagination.

History's wooden fences generally fall into one of two categories: closed-board and open-board. Originally a means of defense against warfare's oncoming hordes, the closed-board fence efficiently fulfills its role as a forbidding, impenetrable barrier. Not among the most ornamental of solutions, planks fitted side by side can be dressed up and the austerity softened by the addition of a border of openwork at the top. Another mitigating factor is height: a three- to five-foot fence is much less ominous than one that scales the heights at eight to ten feet.

A very dear friend of mine, Hope Hendler, lives in a situation that is the envy of most Manhattanites: a ground-floor row-house apartment on the Upper East Side that opens onto a backyard garden. Some years

ago, she telephoned me in desperate straits. It seemed that the owner of the house next door had erected a Spartan stockade fence to divide his property from Hope's. The parterre beds and formal French design of her garden were in jeopardy. What was she to do?

She decided, first of all, to whitewash the seven-foot tall fence's raw wood surface. In an effort to minimize its graceless, overbearing

LEFT, *Resourceful Hope Hendler turned her Manhattan town house plot into a Parisian oasis with the help of an old mirror, which appears to double the size of the garden, and aged, lovingly reconstructed lattice rescued from a neighborhood sidewalk.*

RIGHT, *Hung with new 4'x6' lattice panels flanked by antique fragments, the neighbor's stockade fence became an extension of the French flair of her parterre beds. The lattice provides a home for ivy in winter and morning glories in summer.*

buildings, obviated the need to fasten the panels securely. We opted for hanging them, picture-style, on nails driven into the fence, so that they could be removed easily for future repainting.

The transformation achieved by the lattice appliqué was startling; with a minimum of expense and effort, we turned a sow's ear into a silk purse in short order and gave the garden a lattice surface that

presence, I constructed a series of framed diamond-pattern lattice panels using one-inch-wide lath spaced two and one-half inches apart. Designed to fit neatly between the fence's posts, the panels measured six feet long by four feet high. Hope painted them a blue-green color that would contrast nicely with the white of the fence. The sheltered nature of the garden, surrounded by low-rise

today is home for English ivy all year and lavish bowers of morning glory in summer.

The low, open-board fence that has become a staple in American gardens first appeared in Europe in the 1700s. It was inspired, in large part, by the kinds of balustrades depicted in the Chinese art and artifacts reaching the Western world at the time. Its earliest manifestation in this country is represented by the split rail fence. With boards rough-hewn from whole oak or chestnut logs, this pioneering solution for animal containment was the original proponent of the dictum that form follow function. To

pie, the picket fence actually has its roots in eighth century China and fourteenth century Europe. The combination of vertical pales, or pickets, fastened top and bottom to horizontal railings, has become one

Arriving with our earliest settlers, America's first picket fence was a simple affair: sharpened wooden boards driven into the ground and nailed at the top to a single railing. In no time at all, our

enhance stability, its split rails were frequently laid in a zigzag, rather than straight, line, thus earning the eighteenth century tags, worm and snake.

 Seemingly as American as apple

of the garden's timeless classics. Its joy is well known by children, who prize it for the sound made by a stick dragged along it, and by the rosarians who rely on its support for their prized climbers and ramblers.

Colonial forebears, realizing that contact with soil moisture encouraged rapid deterioration, reversed the design; the pointed ends were positioned at the top and the bottoms were lifted away from the

FAR LEFT, *The heaviness of this house in old Huntsville, Alabama, is lightened by the addition of an ornately cut picket fence with American Gothic-style post finials.*

NEAR LEFT, *Wattle does not last forever, but rather quietly ages and eventually begins to disintegrate, at which time it can be processed for composting. The medium is becoming increasingly popular, as gardeners come to understand the value of recycling. Brush and other prunings that in the past were sent off to the community landfill can now be saved for other uses.*

ground. A second railing was added to hold the pales, or spindles, in place. In this ironic way, a topsy-turvy solution gave serendipitous birth to the American picket fence.

New England picket fences were a reflection of the functional, no-nonsense attitude adhered to by the region's settlers. The classic purity and simplicity of these fences, conceived more as a frame for the yard than as a blockade, have survived the centuries intact to lend warmth and grace to the American landscape. Lovingly preserved and restored over the years, the picket fences at Colonial Williamsburg are

a testament to the elegant refinement the form achieved in the eighteenth century. A visit to this marvelous restoration will go a long way toward helping you decide on a design for a picket fence of your own.

As one would imagine, the nineteenth century Victorian picket fence breathed new life into the concept. With one inventive variation on the theme after another, it embarked on uninhibited flights of fancy. Unadorned picket gates assumed Gothic grillwork, and posts graduated to hefty columns topped with finials, urns, or pineapples (the traditional symbol of hospitality).

But it was the Victorians who also gave us the rustic fence, gingerbread's antithesis. Recycling the countryside's castoffs, these wonderfully natural barriers were early proponents of the waste-not-want-not philosophy. By gathering canes and twigs, or clipping deadwood from shrubs, and crisscrossing or weaving them, either in repeated patterns or free-form, the Victorians devised openwork screens that mirrored the garden's inherent beauty. In many cases, whole branch formations were left intact and positioned to lend their natural form to the fence design.

Lattice fencing of a classic nature ensures that the divide between neighbors will always be a gracious one. This fence defines the border between two town house gardens on the East Side of Manhattan.

From the rustic fence to the lattice fence was an inevitable evolution that took place in this country sometime toward the end of the eighteenth and beginning of the nineteenth centuries. But the lattice fence had already earned itself a distinguished place in history. France's majestic Sun King, Louis XIV, instigated and elaborated the concept as we know it today at Versailles. Louis was an impatient king who demanded instant gratification. The kinds of elaborate garden barriers and structures he envisioned, if made of stone, would be too time-consuming and laborious. So his vast army of workers constructed fences, many as high as twenty feet, fabricated of one-inch, European or sweet chestnut lath (painted green). These were positioned against the hornbeam hedges that enclosed the succession of garden rooms, or *bosquets*, that proliferated throughout the chateau's grounds. Though sometimes fashioned of metal, the fragility of these walls assured their early demise. They are known to us today only through paintings and architectural woodcuts.

In my humble opinion, for sheer ornamental value and versatility, lattice as a fencing medium is without equal. Like a computer-generated graph matrix, its crosshatch screening can be loosened or tightened, depending on whether an area is to be completely hidden from view or a glimpse of it, in varying degrees, is to be encouraged. The lattice can be constructed of an all but endless variety of woods, which have been treated, stained, painted, or allowed to develop a natural patina from exposure to the elements.

Sturdiness is another variable, subject to the builder's desires. Depending on lumber dimensions, a lattice fence can be of lacy delicacy or as strong as a bulwark, forbidding to intruders while supporting the thickest, most gnarled of vine branches. But no matter how powerfully resilient, a lattice fence always has the ability to ornament the garden handsomely.

For the ultimate in strength and permanence, nothing surpasses a fence executed in metal. While costly and demanding in time and craftsmanship, the wrought iron fence has enjoyed a prominent place in history. Reaching its full flowering in Europe during the Renaissance, the form knew no limits in ornate expressiveness, depicting leaves, flowers, and other objects of nature, and sometimes

even embellished with gold. My first glimpse of the main gates at Buckingham Palace in London, with their impeccably maintained gilded accents glinting in the sunlight, left a lifelong impression. These portals are a prime example of the lavishness achieved by such ironwork fantasies, and they are fitting tributes to the glory of the once great British Empire.

With the advent of the Industrial Revolution in the mid nineteenth century, wrought iron yielded to cast iron. Faster and less expensive to manufacture, the casting of molten metal delivered the same design impact as iron forged by hand. As lattice fences made of metal are designed to look as if fabricated of wooden laths, cast iron was an imitation of the more refined art of forged metal.

With the renewed appreciation of craftsmanship brought on by the European *art nouveau* movement in the early twentieth century, hand wrought metal enjoyed a revival. Used sparingly today because of the expense involved, ironwork of some kind is the only appropriate design solution in certain circumstances and is always a dependable means of support for a variety of vining plants.

LEFT TOP, *In another display of metal lattice, this archway is deceivingly sturdy and well protected against the elements for many years to come.*

LEFT BOTTOM, *This door, executed in metal, features a berry and moss covered wreath that takes advantage of natural materials as the year goes by.*

ABOVE, *There is nothing like a very high lattice wall for defining property lines and providing barriers and privacy screening.*

Added strength is gained by the guy wires along the top of this handsome lattice fence at Bourton House in England. The garden is privately owned, but graciously opened to the public from time to time.

THE GATE

The Old English word *gaet* was used for the giant fortress entrances, with moveable openings, that kept invaders from penetrating the confines of medieval castles. The clown in Shakespeare's *Twelfth Night* wisely admonishes, "Gainst knaves and thieves men shut their gates." By the seventeenth century in Europe, gates had graduated to elaborate affairs made of ornate metal filigree and flanked by giant stone piers. Intended as fitting announcements of the opulence within, these were sometimes blessed with downward sloping wing extensions and were regularly topped with hefty urns or finials.

I sometimes find myself thinking of gates as suffering from split personalities. On the one hand, they are invitations to enter and discover what lies within. On the other, they are meant to bar the way, to keep people and animals out. Whether locked or unlocked, a gate, like any other form of garden architecture, can be an ornamental statement that reflects and enhances the design of a garden and the fence that surrounds it. And when a gate joins forces with an overhead arbor, it takes on justification for including

FAR LEFT TOP, *A pleasing contrast between widely spaced lattice with much tighter placement is clearly emphasized in this neoclassic entryway. Large ball finials at the tops of the posts welcome visitors in the grand manner.*

FAR LEFT BOTTOM, *A rustic-inspired gate in the Botanical Garden at the University of British Columbia keeps intruders at bay without surrendering its aesthetic appeal.*

NEAR LEFT TOP, *Beyond these gates lies one of the most magnificent rose gardens in all the United States, maybe the world. The Cranford Rose Garden at the Brooklyn Botanic Garden was designed by Harold Caparn in the 1920s and endowed by Mr. and Mrs. Walter V. Cranford.*

NEAR LEFT BOTTOM, *Lacy ironwork crowns one of the many entrances that welcome visitors to the splendid Hidcote Manor Gardens.*

it here, an ideal home for a climbing plant. There is no more welcoming first impression for visitors than opening the garden gate and passing under a halo of bloom.

Covered gates are not without historical precedent. Gardeners in the Middle Ages favored them, and starting with the sixteenth century, lych gates marked the entrances to English churchyard cemeteries. With commodiously protective roofs, these served to shelter mourners and pallbearers while burial services were conducted.

Pictured on these pages is a sampling of some of the most tantalizing among the world's garden structures through the centuries. I trust they will inspire you as they have me. Today's lattice gardener stands to learn much from a peek at the best of the Old World, from the most grandiose, to the funniest of foibles and follies.

LEFT, *The elegant, half-lap construction technique of these sturdy gates inspires confidence at Longue Vue Gardens in New Orleans.*

The Lure of Lattice

Every gardener who has ever attempted to tame the unruly ramblings of a vining plant eventually comes to the conclusion that the only solution is to provide it with something to latch onto and hold it upright. An instantly accessible arrangement for supporting a vine is a set of four or five narrow bamboo stakes, six to eight feet long, stuck into the ground in a circle and tied together at the top. Borrowing from the ingenuity of Native American tepees, this quick and easy arrangement, an ideal uplift for such vines as clematis, jasmine, and passion flower, makes a delightfully unexpected vertical accent in the garden.

Lattice at its most fundamental, a simple trellis panel, free-standing in the ground or in a pot, or fastened to a wall, is another humble beginning that yields much more than its lowly nature would indicate. With its unassuming arrangement of a few crisscrossing sticks or laths, this is the garden's time-honored basic mainstay, forming an anchor for a vine to latch onto, while allowing space for growth.

Author and photographer Elvin McDonald and I have a garden in Houston. In our zeal to fill it with colorful bloom, we planted a border with purple hyacinth bean (*Dolichos lablab*), rambling roses and passion vine (*Passiflora*). Little did we anticipate that, very quickly, like the mythical man-eating plant, a nasty tangle of growth threatened to suffocate everything in sight.

ABOVE, *The two pyracanthas, painfully trained on lattice panels, were well worth the effort. They displayed extraordinary white blooms and brilliant red berries (sometimes simultaneously).*

With no time to build to my specifications, I motored down to our local home-improvement center. There I found modestly priced, unpainted, ready-made trellises measuring thirty inches by eight feet. Eight of these panels, attached between windows on the house wall that backed the border, gave us what we needed in short order.

Two more panels, attached to the front of the house and flanking a large window, came to the rescue in controlling two wildly overgrown pyracantha bushes. Braving the menacing thorns that cover these shrubs and judiciously pruning selected branches over a period of days in winter, Elvin painstakingly worked what remained into the lattice underpinning. The reward of his intrepid labors proved to be a spectacular show the following spring. The panels at the front of the house were completely covered with virginal white bloom and shiny red berries in a breathtaking simultaneous display.

Our attempt to tame nature was again borrowed from the wisdom of many civilizations before us. Latticework, grillwork, and fretwork, from one ingenious expression to another, has been a steadfast ally of all gardeners throughout history.

THE MIGHTY ROMANS

The glories of the Roman Empire, elaborating on those of the noble Greeks, were reflected in the structures its patrician citizens devised to support ancient shoots and vines. Again, grillwork, usually of wrought iron, was the order of the day. An example of the latticed metal arbors the Romans favored can be seen today at the J. Paul Getty Museum in Malibu, California. This remarkable edifice, designed to house billionaire Getty's celebrated collection of antiquities, is a re-creation, down to the tiniest detail, of the Villa dei Papiri, the befittingly opulent residence of a wealthy nobleman in ancient Pompeii.

Buried by the explosive eruption of Mount Vesuvius in A.D. 79, the villa to this day remains unexcavated. Its proportions and dimensions were revealed by archeologists solely by laborious tunneling. And in its resurrection in Malibu, no expense was spared. In the relentless pursuit of matching its original splendor, there is marble of every hue from various parts of the world, and brass fittings and hand-painted murals abound. Like the phoenix rising from the ashes, the structure as it stands today is awe inspiring.

ABOVE, *At the J. Paul Getty Museum in Malibu, California, swags of living ivy loop from column to column.*

The museum is open to the public, and the first sight to greet the visitor is a truly dazzling one: a luxuriously expansive forecourt with a reflecting pool at its center and a roofed colonnade lining its perimeter. Axial symmetry reigns supreme, and oleanders, roses,

grapes. The sybaritic Romans knew a thing or two, and we could profit immensely by following their lead.

Europeans of the Middle Ages and the Renaissance refined the art of wattling, the basketlike weaving of canes and shoots, to fashion impenetrable barriers. These were a

impeccably manicured boxwood, metal arbors, pergolas, and statuary accentuate the classic formality. On a visit one hot summer day, I strolled under a grape-vine–laden pergola, one of four over walkways in the courtyard, and was suddenly engulfed by a refreshing coolness tinged with the delicious scent of

kind of precursor to lattice. Owing much to the ingenuity of the nest building of birds, this rustic preview of the lattice matrix promised an eye-pleasing solution to an otherwise thorny problem. A good idea yearns to survive the ages, and to this day, the wattle fence can be found throughout the British Isles.

ABOVE, *A metal arch, such as this one, with a lattice back panel, was one of the ways of supporting vining and climbing plants in ancient Rome.*

The Mysteries of the Orient

Completely unaware of developments in the West, the ancient civilizations of Asia fashioned screens and grids with their own inimitable design concepts. Their structures were usually heavily embellished and leaning toward the ornate when made of stone, or a simple celebration of the natural when constructed of bamboo. Japanese tea houses and Chinese pagodas and *t'ings* have been indispensable elements in the landscape for eons, and it would be hard to find a Chinese example without grillwork or apertures of some kind.

A great variety of structures fostered the contemplative nature of Oriental gardens centuries before the idea of a pergola occurred to the early citizens of Rome. Not unlike the English wattle fence, Asian bamboo barriers offer the unfettered, unprocessed beauty of nature itself, while providing unparalleled versatility. Even the traditional fastening material, tied raffia, scoffs at the stringency of hard-bitten nails, screws, and bolts.

The Innovative Dutch

In any examination of the emergence of grandly ornate trelliswork in Europe, credit must be given to the enterprising Dutch. It was in the Netherlands, in the seventeenth century, that the kind of treillage that caught France's Louis XIV's fancy first appeared. In fact, the celebrated garden designer André Le Nôtre, who was responsible for the gardens at Versailles, imported skilled Dutch craftsmen in the 1670s to fabricate elaborate lattice structures for the great chateau Chantilly.

RIGHT, *A bench, or more like a throne fit for a king, was the starting point for this elaborate construction at Het Loo in Holland. The garden was built as part of a hunting lodge for William of Orange and Mary Stuart at the end of the seventeenth century.*

ABOVE, *Lattice, Chinese style, frames a stone and bamboo tableaux at the Dr. Sun Yat-Sen Classical Chinese Garden in Vancouver, British Columbia.*

The garden at Het Loo in the Netherlands, created in the seventeenth century for the Dutch monarch William III, is a fitting tribute to the rarefied lattice repertoire accumulated at one time in the Netherlands. Some very fine lattice restorations can be seen today at this legendary garden. One of them is particularly memorable: a garden bench fit for a king. More like a throne, it sits at the base of a towering lattice wall that celebrates the last word in symmetry. A soaring arch marks its center and two giant scrolls shore up its sides.

Painted a favorite color of mine, a grayish blue-green that bears a kinship to the color of blue spruce, this formidable structure capitalizes on one of latticework's most endearing assets: its ability to combine and contrast various lattice sizes and textures to delineate design patterns and create relief.

From Holland and France in the mid 1600s, the frenzy of formal, monumental treillage eventually infected all of Europe, even making its way to the great woodworkers in Russia, as well as to the New World. But with the advent of the lost interest in elaborate latticework, its use faded somewhat from the scene.

BELOW, *A close-up detail of the heroic lattice structure at Het Loo is a lattice lover's dream, providing insights and inspiration for various patterns, as well as a study of paint colors used to magical effect.*

The Vivid Victorians

It was those lovers of the sumptuously lavish, the nineteenth century Victorians, who were only too delighted to rediscover the myriad attributes of latticework. Lattice became the theme of the age, but with a new twist. Not content with the classical forms that occupied their predecessors, the Victorians infused the medium with balls, spindles, spandrels, curlicue cornices, and the many other runaway embell-ishments that came to be known as gingerbread, the icing on the cake.

The neo-Greco inclinations of America's great southern ante-bellum plantations were a refreshing exception to the Victorian rule. In the gardens and among the gazebos and pavilions of these great houses, many of which survive and are open to the public, classicism prevailed. The noble inclinations of the Old South's aesthetic sensibility seemed an uncanny anticipation of what was to come.

ABOVE, *This remarkable latticework architecture can be found in, of all places, Disneyland, in Anaheim, California. It forms a part of Main Street U.S.A. and represents a Victorian sensibility long since abandoned.*

Classicism Rediscovered

With the dawn of the twentieth century, a curious thing happened. The Western world turned its back on Victorian excess and yearned for the cleaner, simpler aesthetics of design. Nowhere is this more evident than in the catalogs of J. P. White's Pyghtle Works of Bedford, England, a prolific supplier of garden furniture and ornament to homeowners of the early 1900s and to such leading landscape artisans as Jekyll, Lutyens, and Sackville-West.

First appearing in 1910 and collected today in one volume, *Garden Furniture and Ornament* (Apollo), these catalogs illustrate a treasure trove of lattice fences, arbors, gazebos, garden houses, and pavilions, as well as a plethora of gates, benches, and bridges. The designs are decidedly classic, eschewing the froufrou of Victorianism and re-establishing the legacy of the French and the Dutch. This extraordinary collection has become one of my most reliable references. In modern times, we have only begun to scratch the surface of the magnificence in garden architecture achieved in England at the turn of the century.

Palatial Ambitions in America

In America, too, the early twentieth century saw a renaissance in the use of classically inspired lattice. This was the heyday of the robber baron industrialists who dotted the land with palatial manor houses, appropriate monuments to the enormous wealth they had accumulated, seemingly almost overnight. The Carnegies, the Mellons, the Vanderbilts, the du Ponts, and others saw fit to erect elaborate manses that were every bit as impressive as the great villas and chateaux of Europe. Many of these have been lovingly restored in recent years and are accessible to the public, albeit some of them during the summer months only.

Among the lattice surprises to be discovered at these lavish homesteads, two are etched indelibly in my mind. One is a *trompe l'oeil* lattice appliqué at Nemours, the Wilmington, Delaware, mansion designed in Louis XIV chateau style by Carrere & Hastings in 1909 to 1910 for Alfred I. du Pont.

The French formality of Nemours's extensive gardens, completed in 1932, is enormously indebted to this very special lattice

LEFT, *The immense lattice matrix of this structure at Old Westbury Gardens stands out sharply against the evening sky.*

RIGHT, *Designed without a single lapse in aesthetic perfection by Henry A. Crawley in 1910, Old Westbury Gardens will always hold a special place in my heart. The walled Italian garden is an extraordinary habitat. It is the home of one of the grandest lattice pavilions in the world. The raison d'être of lattice pavilions of a certain size and airiness, such as these, are their views from inside. Each aperture frames a tableau of Eden.*

LEFT, *It is imperative that a concrete footing be used to protect every point at which a wooden structure touches the ground. Water accumulation is lattice's greatest menace as it will rot wood very quickly. With these structures at Old Westbury Gardens, great pains are taken to keep the wood dry.*

RIGHT, *The semi-circular pond that fronts the lattice pavilions is stocked with water lilies, koi, and fountains.*

overlay. It covers one entire wall of the house and beautifully frames the formal parterre garden laid out in front of it. The classical arches, false windows, friezes, and columns of the blue-green lattice design— a little of the sublime, elegant majesty

rear facade of a row house in Brooklyn, New York. The columns and friezes I designed in modules of varying lattice textures to overlay two stories of the building's wall, artfully surrounding its windows, made their own very powerful statement.

That particular project, more than any I have been involved with, heavily underscores the native ability of latticework to master the art of illusion, to hide and conceal the unsightly with a generous helping of cleverness and a soupçon of

of French treillage inevitably finding its way to America—lend depth and interest to what would otherwise have been an uninteresting, blank, pink stucco wall.

I blatantly borrowed from this masterful lattice design when I was asked to camouflage the rusticated

Rather than cause for averting the eye, the wall became the handsome focal point for the town house's compact rear garden and the ideal background for its plantings. And it accomplished all of this without in any way betraying the eyesore of crumbling brick that lay behind it.

effort. A more detailed examination of this design's conception, materials, and construction may be found on pages 105–7.

The other turn-of-the-century lattice restoration that will always hold a very special place in my heart proudly stands today at Old

The central pavilion of the structure can be seen in the

distance and the journey to it promises to be a floriferous one.

Westbury Gardens in Old Westbury, on the north shore of Long Island. One of the grandest of this area's industrialist citadels, Old Westbury was among the inspirations for the fictional houses in Fitzgerald's *The Great Gatsby* and has played a prominent role in numerous films and television commercials. In real life, it was once the home of John Shaffer Phipps, son of steel magnate Henry Phipps.

Returning to America with his young bride, Margarita, an English aristocrat, John Phipps was determined to please her by re-creating a bit of England in America. In 1906, he commissioned London-born architect George A. Crawley to design a manor house, with gardens, typical of those built in England during the reign of Charles II in the seventeenth century. Crawley succeeded brilliantly in creating an estate that the proudest of English nobility would gladly call their own.

After vacating a major portion of the estate, the Phipps family established a foundation to oversee its preservation, and they opened it to the public in 1959. Its seventy-two—room main house, filled with English antiques and paintings, its formal and naturalized gardens,

and its sumptuous vistas are enjoyed by thousands of visitors every summer.

While living in New York City, I had the distinct privilege of experiencing this spectacular homestead frequently. Whenever I drove up the long alley of specimen lindens that announced its main entrance and caught my first glimpse of the manor house, I was reminded once again of the impeccable sense of aesthetics that reigns supreme throughout the mansion and grounds. From the grandest gesture to the tiniest detail, not a single lapse in taste can be found. In fact, during my frequent visits to the gardens, sometimes I would feel transported back to merry old England.

Invariably, with each visit, I was drawn like a magnet to one very special feature of the garden, an elaborate lattice structure that curves along the edge of a reflecting pool and handsomely crowns the formal symmetry of the walled Italian Garden. Also of George Crawley's design, this magnificent installation consists of three domed pavilions connected by a pergola-like colonnade. Lovingly preserved and restored by the caretakers of Old Westbury, this amazing structure has survived for almost 100 years. Its thick hardwood members continue ever-faithfully to support some very old wisteria vines, whose generous show of otherworldly lavaliere blossoms in spring is indeed a sight to behold.

A decided Chinese, or *chinoiserie*, influence permeates the design of the latticework. Its debt to the Orient is revealed in the upswinging beams at the bases of its domes, the almost Chinese-Chippendale bent of some of its openwork, its oval cutouts, and the color painted throughout: a blue-green the gardens describes as *bleu de Chin*, a shade only the French would boast a familiarity with. We have to be content merely with a literal translation, Chinese blue.

One of the most gorgeously grandiose treillage examples extant in America today, this installation, both through sheer admiration and by unconscious osmosis, has permeated much of my own work. Attesting to this spiritually symbiotic relationship, at the New York Flower Show, I would often over hear visitors saying, "This must be Old Westbury's," when they first caught sight of the exhibits I designed. Invariably I thought to myself, as I smiled contentedly, the compliment is well taken.

A Rose Garden Grows in Brooklyn

The establishment of the Brooklyn Botanic Garden in 1910 on a former city dump site in Brooklyn, New York, earns it the right to be included here with the baronial likes of Nemours and Old Westbury. Indeed, the garden's administration building, a historic landmark designed by the celebrated McKim, Mead, and White in Italian-Renaissance style, is sited in a manner reminiscent of a turn-of-the-century manor house, this one presiding over fifty-two acres of formal and naturalized gardens.

A miraculous emerald oasis bravely holding its own against a near-explosive urban surround, and a paragon of education, research,

ABOVE, *The 'American Pillar' rose has found a flattering place for its charms on a lattice fence at the Cranford Rose Garden.*

RIGHT, *From the Overlook, a walkway along one end of the garden, one can appreciate the Cranford Rose Garden in its entirety, a little over an acre. The rose-filled, herbaceous borders are at their peak around early June.*

and community service, the BBG will always be a very special place for me. In addition to working briefly in its publications department, I was born in Brooklyn and knew the garden as a baby. Before I could walk, my mother wheeled me in a stroller down its flower-bordered paths. Unfortunately, I left Brooklyn for New Jersey when I was six, so I have no real memory of those idyllic days of communing with nature. But I am certain my mother never sauntered over to the Cranford Rose Garden before we moved, because, as young as I was, I know the sight never would have left me.

A splendid pavilion, a veritable little peaked-roof house of lattice, sits on a rise at the far end of the garden's formal plan. Designed by Harold Caparn in the 1920s, the structure is a textbook study in symmetry and proportion. Oval and square apertures and round columns accenting diamond-and-square–patterned lattice announce its classical, rather than Victorian, ancestors. The design owes much to the seventeenth century Dutch and French, on through the likes of the lattice wall at Nemours and the pavilions at Old Westbury. A glorious vision of overflowing abundance when masses of roses span its openwork roof, this enchanting structure has stood the test of time to become another of my many inspirations.

Often reserved for wedding ceremonies, the Cranford lattice pavilion commands a view of one of the finest rose gardens in the world. The intoxicating, fruity scent of over 5,000 hybrids, species, and old fashioned roses, at the height of bloom in late spring, hold one spellbound, while at the same time, their brilliant pinks, reds, apricots, yellows, whites, and mauves dazzle the eye.

The symmetrical layout of the garden's paths and conscientiously labeled beds, and its charming, almost storybook, setting, offer an expert lesson in the art of training roses. Among the many ingenious means of support at work here are the tall lattice fence that surrounds the garden laden with climbers; the double arbors crossing one another to lift bowers of bloom over pathways; and the festoons, an English invention enlisting poles connected by swags of chain, a kind of tightrope that fearless vines traverse without hesitation.

If you are helplessly stricken with the incurable urge to plant a rose garden, then the Cranford is a must-see site. If for nothing more than to enjoy one of the most exuberant gatherings of roses anywhere, negotiating the nether reaches of Brooklyn will be an adventure well considered.

A source of inspiration to countless gardeners, the Rose Pavilion at the Cranford Rose Garden in the Brooklyn Botanic Garden employs a wide range of innovative structural elements. Featured here is an oval window in a lattice wall.

AN AMERICAN VISIONARY

Almost single-handedly responsible for America's liberation from Victorian fussiness in lattice design was an extraordinary innovator named Ogden Codman. Born in 1863 to a rather well-to-do Massachusetts family, Codman, from the ages of nine to nineteen, was educated in France. Returning to America armed with the extraordinary design traditions of France and with only one year of formal training on this side of the Atlantic, he quickly rose to the stature of interior designer and architect to the wealthy of Newport, Boston, and New York. And it was not long before he forged a lifelong alliance with the novelist and garden designer Edith Wharton, mentioned earlier in this chapter.

It was my extreme good fortune to have attended a retrospective of Codman's work installed in December of 1988 at New York's National Academy of Design. Ironically, the Academy is headquartered in a Fifth Avenue town house that Codman redesigned inside and out in 1914 for the philanthropist Archer M. Huntington. On display was an extensive collection of Codman's meticulously executed renderings and design plans, and a full reconstruction in wood of a lattice fence, with central niche, from one of his original drawings.

It was overwhelmingly apparent to me, as well as to the Academy, that Codman set about cleaning up the excesses of the nineteenth century, while leaping back to French neo-classicism and English and American Georgian styles of the eighteenth century for his primary inspiration. He revived the use of garden lattice in the manner of the great treillage of France and, happily, his influence prevails to this day.

Never previously having set eyes on Codman's work, I was dumbfounded by the clean-lined pediments, columns, and keystoned arches that appeared before me. Uncannily, they resembled exactly the defining elements of my own designs. By what mystical machinations this phenomenon occurred, I will not even begin to contemplate, but my unintended homage to such a master was unnerving, if not inspirational. Suffice it to say, that Codman's vision gave me great joy, affirming what I was persuing in my own work and obliterating any nagging doubts that I was headed in the right direction.

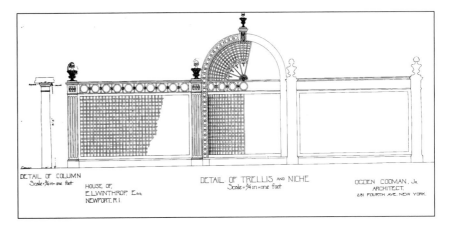

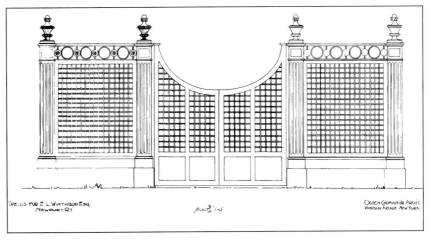

ABOVE, *Two designs from Ogden Codman clearly demonstrate his urge to emphasize a cleaner, bolder design with obvious neo-classic and Georgian influences.*

Fantasy Becomes Reality

"Everything you need to know to build your own" was one of my credos when the idea for this book first took root. A constructional greenhorn at the time, I was scarcely prepared for the vast array of considerations pelled to include in this book all that I have learned through the years regarding materials and construction techniques, so that your decision to hire an expert or to go it alone will be a well-informed one.

Suffice it to say, if you choose to rely on the knowledge and skill of a

The modular fence designed for the 1989 New York Flower show stands today on C. Z. Guest's property.

awaiting the brave soul willing to wield hammer and saw. While it is hardly a problem to find designers and craftsmen all too willing to make real—more than likely at considerable expense—whatever your vision may be, I feel com- professional, what you absorb here will lend you a reassuring measure of confidence when considering design options, negotiating costs, and grappling with the almost endless choices that have a way of relentlessly presenting themselves.

In summer, it is abundantly planted with potted tree-form lantana standards, trained jasmine, and climbing roses.

The Way of All Woods

My initiation into the world of wood construction was an inauspicious one. It marked the revival in 1986, after a fifteen-year hiatus, of the New York Flower Show, and my appointed building site, on wintry weekends, was a series of unheated garages at Templeton, C. Z. Guest's Long Island property. I was given free rein to order whatever I needed from the local lumber yard. Like a delirious child unleashed in Toys 'R Us, I did not stint one bit in making sure I had everything I wanted, and more. That I was limited to rather poor-quality, pressure-treated pine (a serendipitous choice, actually, considering that the structures were destined eventually to weather the out-of-doors) and pieces milled only to standard sizes did not dampen my enthusiasm in the least.

For a carpenter, I was entrusted with one of C. Z.'s retainers, an immigrant from Poland named Tony, who spoke not a word of English, making my task an even greater challenge. Pointing and gesturing was our sole means of communication. All of my design plans, drawn to scale, were laid out before us, and I could only guess at how much of what they represented Tony understood. Often I found myself having to point exactly where to nail and where to saw. And on days when communication broke down completely, there was nothing I could do but take hammer and saw in my very own, less-than-callused, pianist's hands.

From this humble beginning, I went on to implement designs for a series of clients, working with the craftsmen of their choosing. These ran the gamut from carpenters who had not a clue about reading plans, to the finest of cabinetmakers who immediately understood, and sometimes uncannily anticipated (much to my delight), the vicissitudes of my imagination.

Because I was not an expert in the behavior and durability of various woods and the finer points of assembly, I was at the mercy of, and more happily, sometimes indebted to, whatever carpenter I found myself collaborating with. As time went on, I came to depend upon a select group of workmen whose knowledge and understanding proved valuable beyond question, and it was these men I enlisted to participate in more and more of my design commissions. For your own projects, if you decide to hire a professional, be assured of his or her skill and experience. A hasty decision could lead to mixed results. Make an effort to look at this person's previous work, and get reactions from former clients.

One of the most important considerations in the selection of wood for outdoor use is the prevailing weather in the area of the world in which you live. In my recent choice of residence, Houston, for instance, where the humidity is unforgiving year round, only pressure-treated pine or the finest of hardwoods coated with a water-repellent sealant offers the best chance for lasting durability. It is a shame to see a beautiful structure's life shortened on account of poor wood selection.

To help you make an informed choice of the woods that perform acceptably under the conditions of your particular locale, I feel that the most valuable strategy is to offer the personal knowledge of carpenters and builders from various parts of the country. I have had the pleasure of working at some point with all of the craftsmen who follow, and I can assure that each brings to the realm of wood construction years of his special brand of knowledge and experience.

The Northeast

Tim Duval of Plant Specialists in Long Island City, New York, specializing in urban settings including high-rise terraces, has been designing and building lattice installations for at least twenty years. Woods enlisted for the Northeast must withstand the

cent, then it is unsuitable. Tim's *modus operandi* for durability is to prime sufficiently dried wood on all sides, especially cut ends, to help reduce shrinkage over time. He recommends any exterior primer but thinks oil-based paint is best for this purpose.

It is always advisable, when possible, to paint all cut pieces before

LEFT, *Fenced in playground by Tim Duval.*

NEAR RIGHT, *An arched lattice structure echoes and complements a large window elegantly in this New York high-rise setting designed by Tim Duval.*

FAR RIGHT, *Junipers and chrysanthemums find refuge at the base of a very high screen. Lattice lends itself well to height— the higher the screen, the greater the protection from sun and wind.*

extremes of hot, sultry summers and near-Arctic, icy winters, to say nothing of the fearsome winds of skyscraping rooftops.

According to Tim, be sure the wood you want to use is thoroughly dried out before using, especially if it is slated for moldings or other fine detailing. There are devices for measuring water content in wood, and if moisture exceeds ten per-

assembly. Unpainted wood surfaces positioned against each other are a sure invitation for moisture accumulation and deterioration. Tim's ingenious solution for simplifying the painting process is to build a long trough, fill it with paint, and then gingerly dip the laths into it.

An alternative method is "to lay down, side-by-side, one layer (north-south, say) of the laths that will form a particular module, paint that layer, and then nail over it the opposing, east-west layer, and paint it. This technique takes some of the drudgery out of the painting process because you can use an ordinary roller." Incidentally, all of Tim's designs are assembled in modules, a technique favored by most crafts-

men, and advisable for homeowners, to insure rigidity and portability.

The kinds of wood he favors, especially for detail work, are mahogany and teak. Teak is ideal, but the cost is often prohibitive; some mahogany can be found at about the same cost as clear cedar. He finds himself working more and

more with this reliable old standby because it is extremely hard and has a good, clear grain. It also takes paint flawlessly or weathers in the raw to a handsome gray.

After teak and mahogany, Tim's preferences, in descending order, are clear-heart cedar, No. 2 cedar, redwood, and treated pine. He resorts to pine only if it is to be

used raw. Painting brings out its roughness and imperfections too readily, and, like cedar and redwood, it tends to be rather soft. Since these woods show all kinds of

mars and dents easily, he avoids them for high-impact areas such as framing or the edges of planter boxes. For these applications, hardwood is much preferred.

THE SOUTHWEST

"If we had the pine we had sixty years ago, I'd use it today." Daniel Janish of Dan's Custom Woodworking in Houston, Texas, sadly laments the decline over the years in the quality of wood at the disposal of most carpenters. Specializing in fine cabinetry and in the restoration and reproduction of antiques, Dan has been in the business of wood for more years than he can remember.

Like Tim Duval, Dan's preference for outdoor lattice structures is mahogany. Its smoothness and hardness can't be matched, traits that are invaluable, especially in Houston's humidity. And, as in the Northeast, the price is more reasonable, comparable to Western cedar. (Western red cedar, by the way, is actually a misnomer. The tree's real identity is a juniper, its common name a testament to its fragrance, which approximates that of the true cedar.) Dan's list of wood preferences, from the most expensive to the least, stacks up as follows: teak and walnut (which he uses more for furniture), oak (but not for outdoor structures, as it tends to crack), clear-heart redwood, clear-heart cedar, mahogany, Western cedar,

untreated yellow pine (No. 1), and treated pine (Nos. 2 and 3).

For indoor lattice, Dan prefers to use poplar because of its softness and ease of workability. (Poplar is not appropriate for outdoors. It doesn't hold up, especially in the humidity of the South.) Pressure-treated pine is reliable for decks and similar structures, "but," he cautions, "because it splits and has too many imperfections, I don't like

to use it for lattice. The kind available today is just too young." He feels fir is superior to redwood, but it can be too expensive. He also warns that redwood leaches an acid that will corrode ordinary nails. Only bronze or stainless steel nails should be used with this wood.

Dan's litany of available woods seems to preclude all but the hardest and most expensive. For

instance, cypress will do the job, but it has to be tidewater, which is very scarce and therefore very expensive, comparable to teak. Western cedar is acceptable, as long as it comes from the heart of the tree. But according to Dan, the old cedar is mostly gone, and second growth just does not have enough body. "Teak is the king of them all," he sighs admiringly, "and by far the most expensive. Today, it's used mostly in the building of boats and ships, and, in much smaller volume, for fine-quality garden benches that really hold up for years and years."

Dan's preservative of choice, at least for work in the drier parts of the country, is linseed oil. In Houston's humidity, linseed oil mildews and turns black. The best sealant in a humid environment is a couple of coats of house paint. He

LEFT, *With two beautifully constructed trompe l'oeil arches, this lattice screen, constructed of willow by Dan Janish, graces James Steinmeyer's atrium outside of Beaumont, Texas.*

ABOVE, *This naturally aged wooden arbor with seat by Loren Charter displays the wide range of effects that can be achieved by different types of wood.*

also likes to use stains designed for nautical uses. They contain a preservative that keeps them from being bleached by the sun.

Another Houstonian, Loren Charter of Village Woodworks, specializes in the natural look of weathered oak, cypress, cedar, and treated pine for the heavy gates and graceful arbors he custom builds. Although expensive in the Southwest, he also likes redwood, because it is so pleasant to work with, especially for window boxes or containers.

Loren relies mostly on pressure-treated pine for his designs and prefers leaving it unpainted, allowing it to weather naturally. Some of his customers apply a coat of paint or pigmented stain on their own. The only treatment he would use is a clear weatherproof sealant, the kind normally preferred for decks.

Loren points out that the solution used in the pressure-treating process of pine penetrates the wood to a depth of only one to two inches. So the exposed cut ends on some of the heavier lumber, like a 4x4, can pose a problem. On occasion he does what he calls "field treating": he soaks the exposed ends in the treatment solution himself.

To further the natural look and speed up the weathering process, Loren conducted an experiment on one of his designs, an elaborate arbor that serves as a niche for a bench. As he describes it, "We treated the wood with some industrial chemicals. First, we applied tannic acid, then ferrous oxide. The latter you can make yourself by soaking nails in vinegar. When the solution is sufficiently murky with rust, simply apply it to the wood with a brush. The effect is wonderful," Loren says enthusiastically. "Mother Nature couldn't do it any better."

THE MIDWEST

Joe Smiley of Exterior Woodworks in Cleveland, Ohio, is very grateful that he does not have the problem with termites that many other parts of the country have.

For the very fine latticework structures he is well-known for in the environs of Cleveland, Joe mostly relies on select redwood. Cypress is very durable for all areas of the country, he feels, but redwood cannot be surpassed in a midwestern climate. It machines exceptionally well, weathers beauti-fully, and readily accepts paint or stain. His preference for treating redwood is a stain block sealant. "You could classify it as a white shellac. If you'd like a color other than white," he points out, "you have to use paint or a heavily pigmented stain."

Rather than the usual practice of relying on single 4x4s for posts, he laminates two 2x4s or two 2x6s back to back, with the grains opposing one another. This provides much more lasting rigidity than one 4x4, which tends to warp with time.

AVOIDING THE FULL TREATMENT

It is no secret that pressure-treated wood is favored by contractors and home builders alike, because of its relatively low cost and its unsurpassed rot resistance. Yellow pine is the wood of choice because of the nearly blotterlike absorbency of its fibers. The pressure treatment process is as its name implies: lengths of pine are immersed in a tank filled with a liquid preservative under enough pressure to infuse the solution forcibly into the wood.

This arbored enclosure, constructed by Joe Smiley, provides the perfect setting for an overlook at Fellows Riverside Garden in Millcreek Park, Youngstown, Ohio.

The substances most commonly enlisted for this process are the waterborne preservatives, chromated copper arsenate and ammoniacal copper zinc arsenate. Since arsenic is a component of these compounds, they are potentially poisonous. It is essential, when handling treated wood, especially while sanding or sawing, to take the precautions of wearing eye protection, a dust mask, and gloves.

As I have already indicated, all of the structures I designed under the auspices of C. Z. Guest and Elvin McDonald for the New York Flower Show were constructed entirely of pressure-treated pine. The color C.Z. insisted upon for every assemblage was a rich, dark green, approximating the shade purportedly employed at Versailles. An unmixed, standard green house paint was applied to the wood, and despite the objection to the imperfections of treated pine voiced by some of the craftsmen above, I found the results perfectly acceptable, albeit on the rough side if you chose to examine the surfaces close at hand.

Flat, narrow laths in long lengths to be cut for latticework are available at most lumber yards in widths ranging from $3/4$" to $1 5/8$". Bear in mind, however, that, without exception, these are milled of untreated pine and must be thoroughly sealed, painted, or both. This kind of lightweight lath was the mainstay for our New York Flower Show lattice, and it has held up very well, considering it has lived outdoors intact through eight blistering northeastern summers and icy winters.

Preconstructed lattice panels in 4' x 8' and 2' x 8' sizes are available at most home improvement centers, and in these, the laths are treated with a preservative. Since the panels in question come in only two sizes and feature laths that are set at a fixed spacing, creative versatility is not their strong suit. However, as the illustrations in the following chapter reveal, they can be cut to various dimensions and put to all kinds of practical and attractive uses when deftly reassembled.

Treated or untreated, the wood you employ can be further protected from moisture damage if you take the hint passed on to me by some kind soul whose identity I no longer remember. When designing a structure, be sure there will be no part in which water will stand for a time, or from which it will not drain off readily. Cuplike depressions are to be avoided, as are inward facing slopes that thwart instant runoff.

To Paint, or Not to Paint: That Is the Question

Whether to paint the wood of a lattice structure or leave it exposed to the elements to weather naturally to a silvery-gray patina is a question of style and personal preference. Invariably, a suggestion of the rustic is conveyed by raw, weathered wood, and this is the direction to go if it is what you prefer, and especially if it is in keeping with the architectural materials of your house—stone or cedar shingles, say—or its style—Arts and Crafts or contemporary, for example. Craftsman Daniel Janish has found that some woods, such as Western cedar, redwood, fir, and teak, turn gray more readily than others with outdoor weathering.

But for lattice designed for a decidedly formal, traditional setting, painting or staining is almost always the most appropriate solution. A whole rainbow of choices, in keeping with the colors of the elements of your house, is acceptable, but my particular favorites are white, buff, gray, green, and a difficult-to-describe hue that combines soft tones of gray, blue, and green.

While stain normally does not require repeated applications, once you paint, you will have to re-do it periodically. This may be more daunting than it seems because you may have to detach, tendril by tendril, a flourishing vine determined to hang on to its moorings.

Some years ago, a client's town house garden in Manhattan contained a large lattice screen badly in need of painting and repair. Unfortunately, it was covered with English ivy and the choice was to cut it all down or remove it without damage. Lovers of plants that we were and optimists at heart, we opted for the latter. Long hours were spent and much patience was required to roll up each ivy stem as gingerly as possible, repair the lattice, then slowly unfurl the vines to return them to their rightful places. Though the operation was both tedious and extremely time-consuming, scarcely a leaf was lost.

Ripping the Light Fantastic

The lengths of lath described above (those found at lumber yards) measure a mere $1/8$" in thickness. In their favor, these promise an airy appearance and ease of construction; they can be nailed to a frame and fastened at their cross points with a heavy-duty staple gun (loaded with galvanized or otherwise rustproof staples). They yield readily to bending, an asset when it comes to the challenge of shaping arches.

These almost wafer-thin strips leave something to be desired, however, if strength, rigidity, and durability are required. Unfortunately, no other ready-milled lath size is to be found at lumber retailers.

It seems appropriate, at this point, to alert you to the fact that advertised lumber dimensions, 1 x 2, 1 x 3, or 2 x 4, for example, are blatantly misleading. Due to the idiosyncrasies of the milling process, what you choose is not what you get. A 1 x 2, for instance, is actually $3/4$" by $11/2$". All of the others follow suit: a 1 x 3 is $3/4$" by $21/2$"; a 1 x 4 is $3/4$" by $31/2$"; a 1 x 6 is $3/4$" by $51/2$"; a 2 x 4 is $11/2$" by $31/2$"; and a 4 x 4 accurately measures in at $31/2$" by $31/2$". This is an essential consideration when planning a structure on paper. Dimensions can be thrown off substantially if these size adjustments are not taken into account.

For thicker, more substantial lath than the standard ready-made, consider following the lead of professional latticeworkers. To arrive at laths of various thicknesses, use a technique called ripping, which involves cutting various sizes of lumber down their lengths to obtain a thicker, or deeper, lath. For example, an available odd-size wood, referred to as five-quarter, measures a true inch thick (actually $11/16$", to be absolutely precise). By ripping it at depths of $3/8$", $5/8$", or 1", you will end up with a 1" wide lath $3/8$" or $5/8$" deep, or at 1", as deep as it is wide—a true 1" by 1".

Or by ripping 2 x 4s or 2 x 6s, both of whose true widths are $11/2$", you can render laths measuring $11/2$" wide by $3/8$" or $5/8$" deep. These are three and five times, respectively, deeper than ready-made lath. With these more substantial members, much greater sturdiness and latitude of design are available to the lattice gardener. If you do not have a power saw to do it yourself, you will find most lumber yards agreeable to ripping any size wood to the dimensions you specify.

The stark contrast of bare wisteria wood with contemporary sculpture and lattice come together to create a setting of near miraculous beauty.

Judicious Joinery

All of my designs to date have incorporated ready-made or ripped lath, assembled to make lattice by simply overlapping, then nailing or stapling at the cross-points. This is the most expeditious arrangement and one that predominates in the custom and ready-made lattice of modern manufacture.

But in days gone by, when time, skill, and patience were in abundance, carpenters were devoted to the meticulous craftsmanship of flat joinery, where the cross-pieces meet flush, with no overlap. This was achieved by means of a number of time-honored techniques, two of which—half-lap and mortise and tenon—survive to this day.

Half-lap, practiced by craftsman Joe Smiley, among very few others, involves carving out square notches in both of the members to be joined. By fitting the pieces together at the notches and fastening with a waterproof glue, perfectly flush front and back surfaces are ingeniously accomplished.

At the British Museum in London, there is an Egyptian sarcophagus that is estimated to be at least 5,000 years old. The amazing fact that its wooden frame utilizes

half-lap

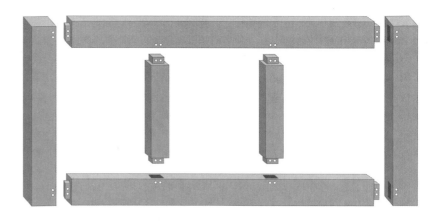

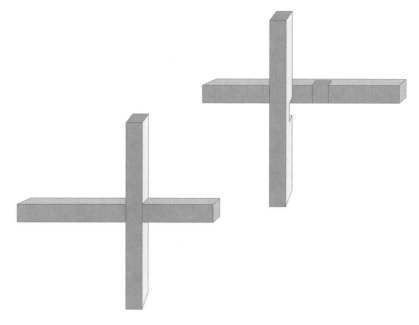

mortise and tenon

mortise and tenon joinery tells us that this carpentry technique has been known and practiced for at least five millennia. It is still relied upon by a small contingent of devoted woodworkers, among them Houston's Loren Charter.

The word mortise (from the Old French *mortoise*) refers to a square-cut cavity (the female component) at the end of a wood cross-piece. The tenon (from the Old French *tenir*, to hold) is an extended square tab (the male component) carved to be fitted into the mortise and held in place with glue, nails, or both. The strength and durability of the joint is unsurpassed in the realm of carpentry, verified beyond a doubt by those resourceful ancient Egyptians.

If it strikes your fancy, test your woodworking skills on these historical joineries. There is a unique sense of satisfaction in discovering the intricate carving of wood strip ends and the snugness and neatness in which they fit together. There is no question that the end justifies the means (no pun intended). Flush joinery is a comely addition to any garden and an ideal foil for vines of every ilk. But overlapped lattice has its own special appeal, one that is accomplished swiftly and easily in the bargain.

KEEPING THOSE FEET DRY

Just as it is essential that water be kept from lingering on any surface of a wooden garden structure, care must also be taken to keep the structure's feet, its support posts, protected from ground soil's lingering wetness. For some of the smaller structures, such as benches and arbors, flat stones or bricks adequately serve to provide dry support at the resting points.

To insure stability for larger structures, however, their posts, no larger than 4x4s in size and preservative treated, ought to be sunk into the ground. Ideally they should rest at a point below the frost line. For nontreated posts, it is advisable to dig a hole (to a below-frost depth) and fill it with concrete. Sink 4x4s and smaller posts directly into the mixture before it has set. Simply rest heavier posts and columns on the concrete's solid surface once it has hardened.

Woodworker Loren Charter offers a helpful hint with regard to con-

crete footings. To borrow more setting time, he mixes crushed limestone with dry Portland cement. With this combination, the setting time is stretched overnight, allowing for repeated adjustments of the position of the post.

Many of the structures that came to rest at C. Z. Guest's estate were slated for already-existing stone or concrete surfaces. To insure permanent stability and moisture protection, my helpmate Tony and I settled on the idea of using galvanized L-brackets to secure the wood to the surface.

At the bottom of a lattice column, for example, we screwed one arm of the L into the wood and the other into the concrete. (There are drill bits made specifically for stone and concrete power drilling.) We fastened the brackets in such a way that the column was lifted off the stone surface just a bit, about an inch. In addition to a measure of air circulation, the tactic guaranteed that the wood would escape the ravages of water accumulation.

LEFT, *Two examples displayed here illustrate the basic construction techniques that dominated lattice construction prior to the advent of prefabricated lattice. Both techniques allow for flush overlaps and cleaner, more precise overall structure.*

DIAMONDS IN THE ROUGH

The diametric opposite of finely wrought latticework is the time-honored technique of enlisting unaltered twigs, boughs, logs, and limbs to create structures of a decidedly rustic bent. A delightful celebration of nature in all its wondrous form and variety, this style of garden architecture is enjoying as much popularity of late as the more formal expression of traditional latticework.

David Robinson, whom I originally met at the first New York Flower Show I was involved with, is a widely-known specialist in the design and building of these raw-branch structures. Now based in Pennington, New Jersey, David was a long-time resident of New York City. He coordinated the recent restoration of all of Central Park's rustic structures, no mean feat considering the number and variety that complement the park's settings.

"Without fail, the first question people ask me," David reflects, "is, where do I get the wood I use in my designs. As a result of my work for the park, I made quite a few connections for sources." David would go to upstate New York, often on field trips to collect raw cedar logs cut

LEFT TOP, *A rustic arbor has all the attributes of a classic one. Interestingly enough, it was a Victorian contingent who sparked the interest in this Arts and Crafts form.*

LEFT CENTER, *A whimsical adornment backs a garden bed at Mohonk Mountain House. Most of the fun and challenge of rustic architecture is in the finding and matching of woods and shapes.*

LEFT BOTTOM, *The ultimate effect in rustic architecture is to utilize a plant in living form. Here, in a design by Edwina Van Gal, wisteria trunks cling to the support of sturdy wooden beams.*

RIGHT, *One of David Robinson's grandest efforts is this cupola-topped pavilion, warmed with golden hues from the setting sun.*

from live specimens. He sought the help of state and county forestry departments for the whereabouts of discarded boughs and branches, and he recommends these institutions as good starting places for beginners.

His work commissions have allowed him the opportunity to collect good materials. For example, he designed a gazebo as part of the conversion of a former private estate into a public park. This was along the Hudson, about ten miles from Olana, the old stomping ground of the Hudson River Valley painters. Locusts and red cedars, ripe for pruning, were in abundance on the property, and he was in seventh heaven.

The kinds of woods David favors are red cedar, locust, mountain laurel, and rhododendron. "The narrow twigs of the last two," he offers, "are ideal elements for a structure's finer embellishments." Mostly he relies on woods that are the most durable for outdoor use. For instance, he discovered that cedar trees growing compactly in stands will have more dense heartwood than those living in open meadow.

The highly durable wood he swears by lately is osage orange. There is a lot of it growing around Princeton, where David lives. It can

be found all over the Midwest and it is indigenous to Oklahoma, Arkansas, and Texas. It is sometimes called hedge apple because of its knobby, bright green fruit, and Native Americans in these territories made bows from its shoots.

With these kinds of naturally durable woods, preservatives are unnecessary. But he does depend on a water repellent, such as Thompson's Water Seal or other similar products, for joining sur-

faces. When securing one log to another, he uses galvanized, sometimes stainless steel, nails, bolts, and screws. Carriage bolts, with rounded heads, are especially good for biting hard into the wood.

David emphasizes that he starts with a plan on paper for most of his structures, a wise decision for anyone contemplating an original design of this nature. Without a drawing it is impossible to know the amount and sizes of the wood you will need. For the major support elements of a structure, he usually selects pieces that are as straight as he can find. But you should not be inflexible, he cautions, as sometimes the shapes of the limbs you collect will dictate the design. You have to keep an open mind and leave some room for spontaneity.

This rustic pavilion, almost classic in its symmetry, was designed in red cedar by David Robinson.

"It's interesting," David notes, "how some clients want the structure to look as wildly natural as possible, while others prefer a more refined approach. Tastes run the gamut, and I like the fact that this special medium of mine can accommodate them all."

THE BAMBOO BOON

The popularity of bamboo is growing by leaps and bounds, as more
and more home gardeners discover
the mysteriously profound beauty of
fences, screens, and other structures
made of the remarkable woody
stems of this giant grass. More
casual in style than lath-made lattice, but not quite as free-form as
the rustic approach, bamboo latticework has a graceful and spiritual
character all its own.

And a garden embellished with
touches of bamboo need not pro-
claim that it is a Japanese garden.
An eclectic mix of styles is more
the order of today; a bamboo
assemblage, while it clearly pays
homage to the Japanese style of
landscaping, can take its place
proudly, fitting in smoothly with
other elements of the garden.

TOP, *Young bamboo shoots grow
alongside painstakingly wrought fences
of cut bamboo.*

CENTER, *The intricacy and variety in
texture that can be created with jute-
tied bamboo shoots is almost infinite.*

BOTTOM, *This particular example
of bamboo artistry recalls the woven
nature of wattling.*

To espalier an oak-leaf hydrangea (*Hydrangea quercifolia*) we were given by a friend a few seasons ago, Elvin McDonald constructed a large (8' x 10') bamboo lattice against a mostly shaded outside wall. This particular species does not require all-day sun, so we thought we had selected the right spot for it.

Pruned to favor long canes that were tied to the lattice, the plant flourished initially, even flowered a bit, but in time, it settled into a kind of unchanging malaise. The bamboo, however, weathered the months admirably, and to this day it ornamentally makes up for what the hydrangea never quite achieved. Elvin has been the world's biggest fan of bamboo trellis work ever since.

Slender bamboo canes, available at most garden centers, are ideal for staking all kinds of flowers and

LEFT, *Bamboo rods provide an aesthetic of their own. This dense grouping will one day support tomatoes, peppers, or cucumbers at Rosemary Verey's Barnsley House.*

vegetables. Crisscrossed and secured with raffia (also found at garden centers), the material becomes the perfect lattice candidate. Slender canes can lend support for potbound vines, while more substantial, thicker stems can be fashioned into screens that are able to support a wide spectrum of heavy-growth varieties.

The famed English author and gardener, Rosemary Verey, makes extensive use of bamboo stakes and arbors in her vegetable and kitchen gardens at Barnsley House in Gloucestershire. The supports take on a decorative life of their own, far beyond the practical consideration of directing and guiding the growth of pole beans, cucumbers, eggplants, peppers, and tomatoes. Not only are the vegetables ornamental in their own right, but so are the little forests of bamboo canes that rise among them.

RIGHT, *Rosemary Verey, one of the world's most knowledgeable plantswomen, set this practical and serviceable bamboo arbor in the kitchen garden of Barnsley House.*

HARDWARE AND FINISHING TOUCHES

It would be heartbreaking to have taken great pains to paint or stain a custom-designed lattice structure, or to have patiently awaited the chameleon transformation of natural weathering, only to have it marred by ugly rust streaking. This is the inevitable outcome of relying on standard-variety metal fastenings, and a tragedy that is easily preventable.

The pristine perfection of structural surfaces may be maintained for years, not by endless repaintings, but by making certain that all hardware materials, whether hinges, latches, staples, nails, screws, or bolts, are made of rustproof material —galvanized aluminum, stainless steel, brass, or concrete-coated metal.

The architectural finishing touches, the diminutive decorative embellishments of any design, include pole-topping finials, moldings, S-curves, and an endless variety of imaginative add-ons. These take on the role of a structure's crowning elements, the special features that have the power to transform it magically from the patently ordinary to the proudly majestic.

ABOVE, *Everything is in the details. These S-curves, which I first saw in a cottage in France, became one of my dearest mainstays.*

When Tony and I were building the fence featured on pages 134–36, I felt its poles were begging to be topped off with slender urn-shaped finials. At the time, I had no idea where to find such creatures. But after scouring the canyons of Manhattan and ending up in, of all places, the fabrics and draperies district of the Lower East Side, I found what I needed.

The hardwood finials that are customarily screwed into the ends of drapery poles can be found in classic urn shapes. Used in vertical stance, rather than the usual horizontal, they suited my purposes handsomely.

They were available in just two sizes: $2\frac{1}{2}"$ and $3\frac{1}{2}"$ in diameter. Amazingly, the $2\frac{1}{2}"$ size was exactly right for perching at the top of the four 3x3 poles that form the closures of the fence's two gates, and the $3\frac{1}{2}"$ size had the precise proportions necessary for the eight 4x4s that support the fence at intervals and the two pairs that flank the main gate.

Providence was shining warmly on me during those frantic days of

having to come up with comely solutions with not a minute to spare. The most beneficent of ornamental benedictions can be yours, too. Drapery ends work surprisingly well, and are very affordable. Another source of inexpensive hardwood urn-and-ball finials (in diameters of $2\frac{1}{2}"$ and 3") is the home improvement center. I have noticed that these and other finishing touches suitable for lattice architecture are becoming available in an ever-increasing number and variety at those enormous home rebuilding chains that are rapidly linking one end of the country to the other.

But if something more customized or original is to your liking, there are skilled woodworkers, certainly those with power lathes, who will turn finials, balls, and poles in an infinite number of shapes, including your own design. Bear in mind always that the more custom workmanship involved, the greater the cost. Refer to the Architectural Sources section at the back of this book for mail-order distributors of quality hardware and decorative trim.

RIGHT, *Every one of these finials may be purchased at local home improvement centers. The selection available has broadened widely in recent years.*

Designs
to Trigger the
Imagination

There is an old maxim that if a design looks good on paper, it will look good in actuality. Drafting with pencil before any work is begun is a rule of thumb I have followed for every one of my designs, and it has never failed me, as long as the drawing has been accurate in every way at the outset. This does not mean I am not still amazed and delighted each time my blueprint makes the almost supernatural metamorphosis into a full-blown structure. I suppose my faith in the process is still a little less than unwavering.

More than helping visualize the projected design, as well as facilitating alterations until they meet with your approval, a drawing acts as a game plan, a map that will direct and assist your carpenter or contractor. To ensure accuracy of dimensions and scale, always draw on graph paper with a ruler and pencil. The squares on the paper are printed to coincide with fractions of an inch, $1/8$" or $1/4$" on a side being the normal standard. To each square you would assign a larger dimension (usually $1/2$" to 1') to translate the rendering's proportions to the assemblage's actual size.

TRELLISES, LYRES, PILLARS, AND FESTOONS

The simplest expression of lattice and a good starting point for any budding latticeworker looking to test his or her mettle is the small trellis, perhaps one for a container plant. Available candidates for the job are tomato stakes, bamboo canes, wooden skewers sold for grilling shish kebab, lumber yard lath, and twigs pruned from shrubs and trees. Also, lumber retailers stock 48"-long round dowels (easy to cut) that range in diameter from $1/4$" to $1/2$".

Illustrated are some suggested grid patterns. But the field is wide open. Any design your imagination can conjure will be workable, as long as it provides appropriate foot-

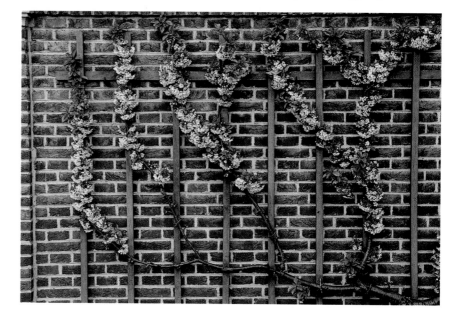

LEFT, *A climbing hydrangea is on its way to becoming a splendid espalier.*

RIGHT, *Even in a provincial little town in France, lattice, with its own special insouciance, may be found.*

BELOW, *Here are suggestions for making a variety of lattice trellises. When making a trellis, let your imagination run rampant.*

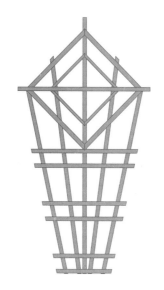

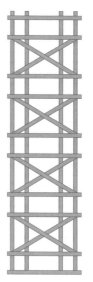

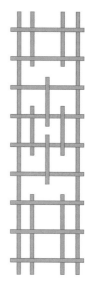

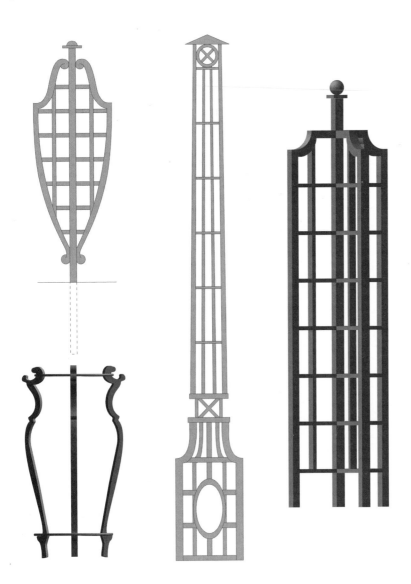

LEFT, *It was tradition in Victorian America to use lyres and pillars to support the growth of a single rose bush. It is an idea whose time has come full circle. These simple, attractive structures can be constructed out of wood or metal.*

ing for the vine to be grown on it. Space support members closely for delicate vines, such as a miniature ivy or rose, and widely for such sturdier varieties as allamandas or passifloras. Depending on the thickness of the cross-pieces, they can be secured to each other with nails, staples, or raffia.

Lyres and pillars from a bygone age, examples of which are shown here, were designed specifically to support roses. With the ever-increasing popularity of this flower, the time seems ripe for a revival of these graceful supports. And certainly this country could use more of the festive fun of festoons. This is what the British call an arrangement of poles with a chain or heavy rope slung between them. Vining roses gradually make their way up the poles and across the ropes. A whole series of poles connected to each other in this way lends the garden an impressive ornamental statement.

ABOVE, *Naumkeag, once a private estate and now open to*
the public, is a paean of the work of the famous landscape architect,
Fletcher Steele. Noteworthy here are the festoons that
embrace one of the house's terraces. Empty now, they could
provide a sturdy support for climbing roses.

Native American Know-How

One of the easiest, fastest, and most useful supports for a wide variety of vining plants is the tripod (having three legs) or quadripod (having four legs). This is the use of three or four stakes of the same length set in the ground, then drawn together and fastened at the top. Once this armature is clothed with a leafy, flowering, sociable climber, it will resemble the familiar American Native dwelling known variously as a tepee or a wigwam, hence its nickname.

A tepee is an ingenious and practical way of achieving verticality in an otherwise flat garden bed. Its size can run the gamut from 8' tall for clematis in the ground to 18" for small-leaved ivies in a 6" pot. Bamboo canes and tomato stakes are often sold in 6' lengths. If four are inserted 5" to 12" into the earth at the corners of a square of ground measuring 18" on a side, the result is a quadripod standing around 5' high.

If a vine is already established, a tepee may be installed over it. Otherwise, transplants may be set or seed sown around the periphery

of the enclosure. A 5' tepee will accommodate almost any young vine for a season or two.

For a tribal-size tepee, use sturdy, relatively straight branches at least an inch in diameter, and set them 8" to 12" into the ground for stability. Purple hyacinth bean vine

will make quick cover in summer, as will butterfly pea vine and Malabar spinach. To help vines find enough foothold, tie garden twine around the tepee, stake to stake, from top to bottom. The twine will give plenty of additional support for the vine's clambering.

BEST VINES FOR TEPEES

Actinidia

Allamanda

Antigonon (coral vine)

Basella (Malabar spinach)

Bignonia (cross vine)

Bougainvillea

Campsis (trumpet vine)

Clematis

Clerodendrum (bleeding-heart vine)

Clitoria (butterfly pea vine)

Dioscorea (cinnamon vine)

Dolichos
(purple hyacinth bean vine)

Gelsemium (Carolina jasmine)

Hedera (English ivy)

Ipomoea (morning glory;
moonflower; cypress vine)

Jasminum (jasmine)

Lathyrus (sweet pea)

Lonicera (honeysuckle)

Mandevilla

Merremia (Hawaiian wood rose)

Millettia (evergreen
wisteria)

Pandorea (bower plant)

Parthenocissus (Boston ivy)

Passiflora (passionflower vine)

Rosa (pillar/rambler and
climbing roses)

Senecio (orange-glow vine)

Solanum (potato vine)

Stephanotis (Madagascar jasmine)

Stigmaphyllon (butterfly vine)

Trachelospermum
(confederate jasmine)

Wisteria

ABOVE, *A stick tepee in C. Z. Guest's garden provides structure for an explosion of sweet autumn clematis.*

LEFT, *A bamboo tepee covered with clematis adds a note of verticality to C. Z. Guest's kitchen garden.*

From Couture to Ready-to-Wear

The ready-made 4'x 8' and 2'x 8' lattice panels that have been on the home front for some time now, have in the last few years enjoyed a noticeable upgrading in quality, choices of woods, and lath spacing. For quite a while, the consumer in search of the look without the labor was faced with only one choice, a rather inelegantly coarse panel made of $1^1/_2$"-wide by $^1/_8$"-thick treated pine laths. The configuration was always the same: a diamond lattice pattern with laths spaced on $4^1/_4$" centers.

For certain utilitarian purposes, these filled the bill adequately. But whenever I came upon all-too-pervasive feeble attempts to use them decoratively, I could not keep from bemoaning the fact that they just did not work, invariably looking awkwardly unfinished. The reason for this was that very few people ever bothered to frame out the panels, to cover over the edges, or the ungainly ends of the laths. Without this finishing procedure, it was impossible to accomplish smoothly the abutment of one panel to another.

In the past, I recommended nailing on lengths of 1x2s or 1x3s

around the perimeter of every panel, no matter how it was to be integrated into a design. But this is no longer necessary, because the lumber industry has at last come to the rescue of the homeowner. Wherever the panels are sold, 8' lengths of grooved molding designed specifically to embrace

the lath ends are available. They have shown up in two convenient versions: a 2"x 2" U-shaped molding for edging the panels and a 2"x 3" H-shaped molding for joining them.

Happily, there are now a number of kinds of lattice panels to choose from, as well. In addition to the

original one, there are: prepainted white or unfinished, treated "heavy-duty" versions with 1½"-wide by ³⁄₈"-thick laths (three times sturdier than the first panels available); "premium" cedar panels with 1½"x¹⁄₈" laths; and "privacy" panels with more tightly spaced laths (on 2½" centers). These all have the diamond configuration, but at long last, there is a square version with laths running horizontally and vertically. These are labeled heavy duty, with 1½" by ³⁄₈" laths spaced on 1¼" centers.

Thoughtfully cut, framed and fitted together, much can be accomplished with these already assembled components. They may be applied to walls or joined to form fences and screens. They may even be used to create structures. As prefabricated lattice becomes more durable and accessible, we can only imagine the possibilities. Illustrated here are some suggestions for enlisting their convenience,

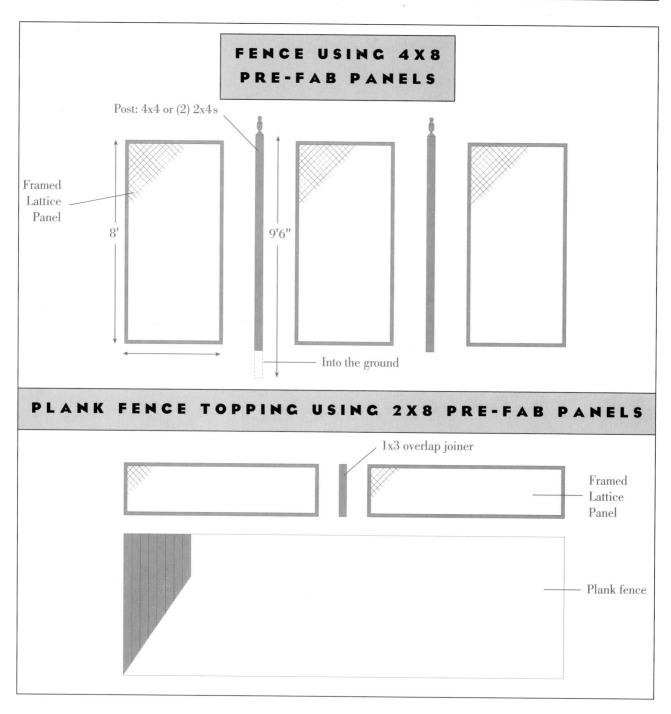

FENCE USING 4X8 PRE-FAB PANELS

Post: 4x4 or (2) 2x4s

Framed Lattice Panel

8'

9'6"

Into the ground

PLANK FENCE TOPPING USING 2X8 PRE-FAB PANELS

1x3 overlap joiner

Framed Lattice Panel

Plank fence

practicality, and attractiveness into your garden.

And if you'd really like to be on the cutting edge of prefabricated lattice, try the new poly-plastic, fiberglass-reinforced, diamond-pattern panels. Available in white, in the same size specifications as the original treated pine panels, and with their own moldings for framing, these are promised by the manufacturer not to rot, mildew, split, or crack. No painting or maintenance of any kind will ever be required, and termites assuredly will not find them palatable.

ABOVE, *The opportunities for construction, using the 2'x8' and 4'x8' ready-made lattice panels available at most lumber yards and home improvement centers, are growing in variety and quality, allowing consumers hands-on creativity and greater latitude.*

Seeing Is Not Always Believing

Of all of latticework's many and varied talents and abilities, one of the most endearing is its capacity to fool the eye. *Trompe l'oeil* (French for deceive the eye) has been a beloved treillage sleight-of-hand contrivance for as long as the medium has been in existence. Closely related to the deception of set design, this aspect of lattice wields a special fascination for me, undoubtedly because of my great love of the theater.

Trompe l'oeil endows a flat, featureless wall, or surface of any kind, with the eye-catching interest of relief. Windows, doors, arches, and columns magically appear where there were none before. One of the most intriguing lattice illusions that has been a favorite throughout the ages is the disappearing perspective. A configuration in which a series of arches grows progressively smaller toward the center, this bit of trickery teases the eye into believing it is gazing down a long gallery.

As mentioned in the first chapter, clients of mine, a young married couple, acquired a run-down row house in an area of Brooklyn

undergoing renewal. More interested in creating a garden in their backyard parcel than in restoring the building, they realized that nothing they could plant would detract from the ugly, rusticating brick of the house's rear facade. With minimal materials and

expense, I covered two stories of the building with lattice in the classic mode. Columns, friezes, and panels of varying textures were attached in modules around the windows by means of cleats, 1-inch-wide wood strips screwed into the softening brick. The panels, in turn, were screwed into the cleats. The illusion was so effective, the transformation so startling—a beauty makeover, as it were—that *House Beautiful* magazine published before and after pictures of the project.

Happening upon this coverage, another client summoned me to a newly acquired Fifth Avenue ground-floor duplex. The apartment

It was true that no matter how beautiful the garden, it would always be overshadowed by that towering wall. As you can see from the unsightly bare facade, this was my greatest design challenge to date. The solution I arrived at was an 84'-long by 27'-high building facade, with columns, false-perspective niches and gallery, a portico, and other neoclassic elements.

LEFT, *A corner of a public space in Paris is enhanced by a finely wrought overlay of lattice. The elements of the lattice suggest the features of a real arcade.*

NEAR RIGHT, *The rear facade of this battered Brooklyn brownstone was obviously in need of some refurbishment. The garden space of the building was the first priority for the house's new, young occupants. Instead of repointing the brick and overhauling the entire wall, they opted to cover the wall with lattice after hearing a lecture of mine at The New York Botanical Gardens.*

FAR RIGHT, *The rear of the brownstone was transformed by the application of the lattice panels I designed for it.*

opened onto a large garden, a rarity in Manhattan, owing to the fact that a neighboring town house had been razed some years ago. But opposite the duplex running the length of the garden was a huge wall covered with black tar, the side facade of the next building. The client was anxious to have it covered as soon as possible.

Two existing windows in the wall, one above the other, were incorporated into one end of the design, and for symmetry, matched at the other end by two false windows. The result was fantastic—proving once again the versatility of this magical medium. This modest proposal is an example of trompe l'oeil at its ultimate.

Bringing the Outdoors In

Some fifteen years ago, I had the privilege of meeting the celebrated designer and photographer Sir Cecil Beaton. Ushered into his presence in the drawing room of Reddish House, a charming sixteenth century cottage in Broad-chalk near Salisbury, I was greeted by a very grand personage carefully posed at the fireplace with one hand resting on the mantle. He had had a minor stroke some time before, but the power of his mind and the radiance of his artistic sensibility were undimmed.

Among the wonders of Reddish House that he proudly revealed to me was a collection of yew topiaries. Each was carved into a whimsical shape that had presided over the garden for some 500 years. But more to the point of the subject at hand was a sunny glass conservatory lined with latticework. It was one of my first exposures to the medium, and its charm and beauty and powerful sense of a garden brought indoors left a lasting impression.

Very much an extension of the *trompe l'oeil* concept, lining the walls and ceilings of indoor spaces with lattice instantly evokes a gar-

NEAR RIGHT TOP, *It is difficult to believe that this space was once an oily, greasy service station. It was taken over by Cleveland florist Don Vanderbrook, who turned it into a lattice fantasy.*

NEAR RIGHT BOTTOM, *The entire ceiling of this dining room in Laguna Beach is fashioned of lattice. With an outer overlay of clear plastic panels, the play of light is fascinating.*

FAR RIGHT, *The owners of this grand pool and atrium in Houston used lattice to embellish and fill in the huge expanses of wall.*

den setting. By no great stretch of the imagination, you can almost feel the caress of summer breezes when enveloped by such an indoor space. Consider enhancing the illusion by growing vines in containers and training them onto the lattice.

light in without enclosing ths space.

One of the great delights of indoor *trompe l'oeil* is that it need not be executed with real materials. Painted expressions—of landscapes, skies, follies, and, yes, lattice—lend the illusion of distant

Good choices for low-light tolerance are ivies and pothos. And lath of the narrow, delicate variety would be the most appropriate for the spatial proportions of the average house's enclosures as it allows

vistas, transforming a tiny space into a vast countryside. Your dearest vision of paradise, no matter how elaborate, can be yours with skillful flourishes of brush and paint.

23"

7'6"

6'

4 ³/₄" 9 ¹/₄"

20"

46"

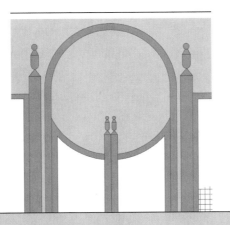

Ready–to–
Build
Design Plans

The architectural plans that make up the extent of this chapter were designed to familiarize you further with basic construction techniques. Ranging from the relatively simple, to the elaborately challenging, they offer you the option of building them yourself, or presenting them as road maps to the contractor of your choice. Mostly modular in concept, they are also meant to be sources of ideas. You need not build the whole structure to glean from it elements that suit your own special purposes.

All building components are derived from standard size lumber. All dimensions are delineated, and wherever possible, a list of sizes and amounts of wood required accompanies the diagrams, all of which are drawn to scale.

I like the idea of combining an arbor with a swing. These grace the Callaway Gardens, in Pine Mountain, Georgia.

An Ornamental Focal Point with Vining Support

Inspired by the classic obelisks of Egypt and Rome, this 7'-tall structure can stand on its own as a striking ornamental element within a bed, or matched with another, the pair can flank an entryway, gateway, or arbor. But its *raison d'être* is much, much more—a home for a vining container plant.

The upper assemblage merely rests on four wooden balls, and, being relatively lightweight, it is easily removable. A potted plant—ideally a rose, but any small vining plant will work—may be sunk into its Versailles-style tub, the obelisk returned to its resting place, and the vining growth gradually worked into the lattice.

The ovals and circles may be cut with a power jigsaw from 1/2" marine-grade plywood or fiberboard. Be sure to seal the edges against moisture with Plastic Wood or some kind of caulking material.

The planter box forming the obelisk's base was inspired by the classic container devised eons ago for Louis XIV's orangerie at Versailles. It is an easy building project if you follow the step-by-step diagrams included.

On the landscape, the lattice shines as an ornament and focal point in its own right. It needs no roses to lend it legitimacy.

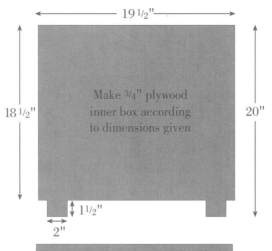

Make ¾" plywood inner box according to dimensions given

19 ½"

18 ½"

20"

1½"

2"

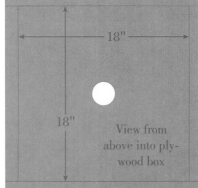

18"

18"

View from above into plywood box

Cut drainage hole in 18"x18 ¾" plywood bottom

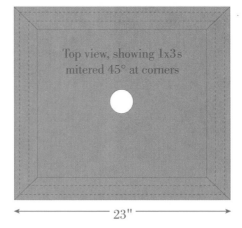

Top view, showing 1x3s mitered 45° at corners

23"

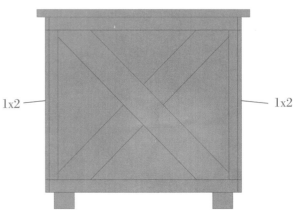

1x2

1x2

LATTICEWORK OBELISK AND VERSAILLES-STYLE PLANTER BOX

This obelisk provides an attractive yet practical addition to the garden. The lattice section merely rests on the four balls of the Versailles-style container beneath it and can be removed with ease. By removing the lattice section, a growing pot can be sunk into the Versailles tub, replacing the lattice, and the vines of the plant can be worked through the obelisk.

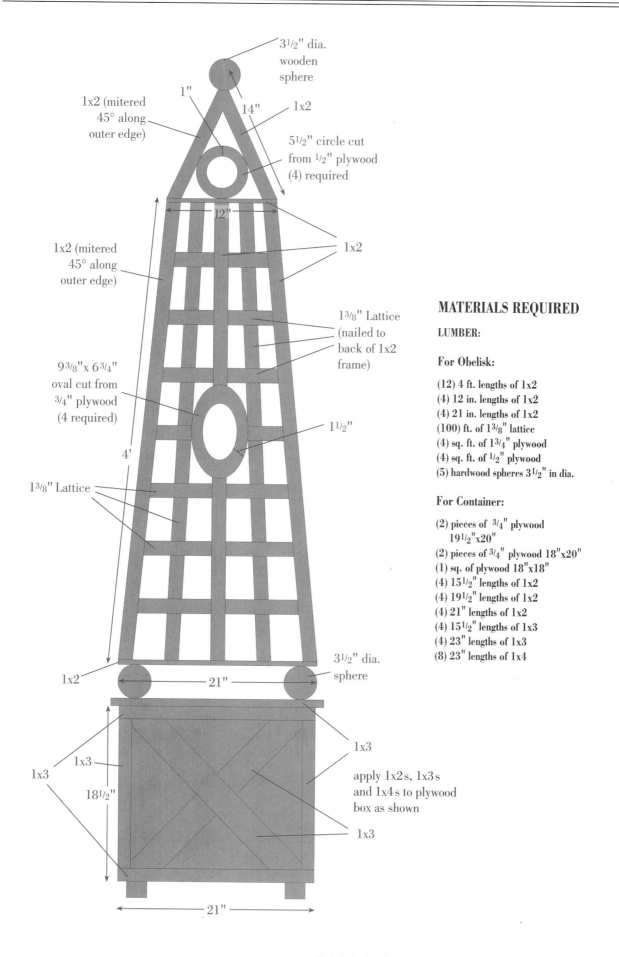

3½" dia. wooden sphere

1"

1x2 (mitered 45° along outer edge)

14"

1x2

5½" circle cut from ½" plywood (4) required

12"

1x2

1x2 (mitered 45° along outer edge)

1⅜" Lattice (nailed to back of 1x2 frame)

9⅜"x 6¾" oval cut from ¾" plywood (4 required)

1½"

4'

1⅜" Lattice

1x2

3½" dia. sphere

21"

1x3

1x3

18½"

1x3

1x3

apply 1x2s, 1x3s and 1x4s to plywood box as shown

1x3

21"

MATERIALS REQUIRED

LUMBER:

For Obelisk:

(12) 4 ft. lengths of 1x2
(4) 12 in. lengths of 1x2
(4) 21 in. lengths of 1x2
(100) ft. of 1⅜" lattice
(4) sq. ft. of 1¾" plywood
(4) sq. ft. of ½" plywood
(5) hardwood spheres 3½" in dia.

For Container:

(2) pieces of ¾" plywood 19½"x20"
(2) pieces of ¾" plywood 18"x20"
(1) sq. of plywood 18"x18"
(4) 15½" lengths of 1x2
(4) 19½" lengths of 1x2
(4) 21" lengths of 1x2
(4) 15½" lengths of 1x3
(4) 23" lengths of 1x3
(8) 23" lengths of 1x4

Snuggling Amid Flower and Fragrance

An arbor-covered bench is everybody's ideal place to relax and contemplate the beauty of the garden. Its greatest asset is its ability to sustain its occupant with the pleasure of close-up flowers and their fragrance.

While the following plan is for a rectangular, flat-topped structure, a curved arbor can also be constructed (see rough plan on page 110 and photograph on pages 128–29). The curve can be achieved by hammering nails into plywood in a pattern that duplicates the curve of a half circle. With the nails holding it in place, bend a 1"-wide lath to form the arc. To this, glue additional layers of lath, one inside the other, until the desired thickness, perhaps 2" or 3", is achieved.

The rose garden at Bellingrath Gardens in Mobile, Alabama, features a number of these inviting little resting places. They offer sociability, not to mention shelter, from the blistering heat of summer.

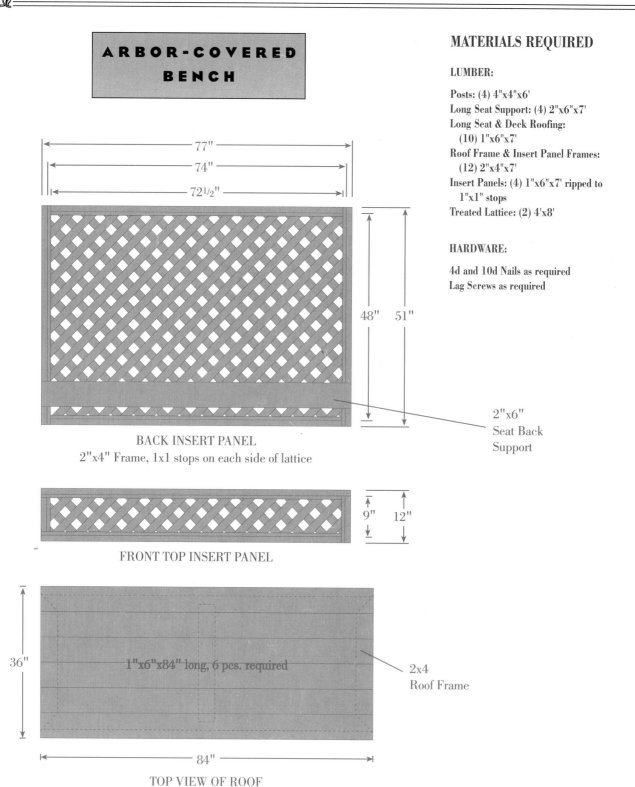

ARBOR-COVERED BENCH

77"

74"

72½"

48" **51"**

BACK INSERT PANEL
2"x4" Frame, 1x1 stops on each side of lattice

9" **12"**

FRONT TOP INSERT PANEL

36"

1"x6"x84" long, 6 pcs. required

2x4
Roof Frame

84"

TOP VIEW OF ROOF

2"x6"
Seat Back
Support

MATERIALS REQUIRED

LUMBER:

Posts: (4) 4"x4"x6'
Long Seat Support: (4) 2"x6"x7'
Long Seat & Deck Roofing:
   (10) 1"x6"x7'
Roof Frame & Insert Panel Frames:
   (12) 2"x4"x7'
Insert Panels: (4) 1"x6"x7' ripped to
   1"x1" stops
Treated Lattice: (2) 4'x8'

HARDWARE:

4d and 10d Nails as required
Lag Screws as required

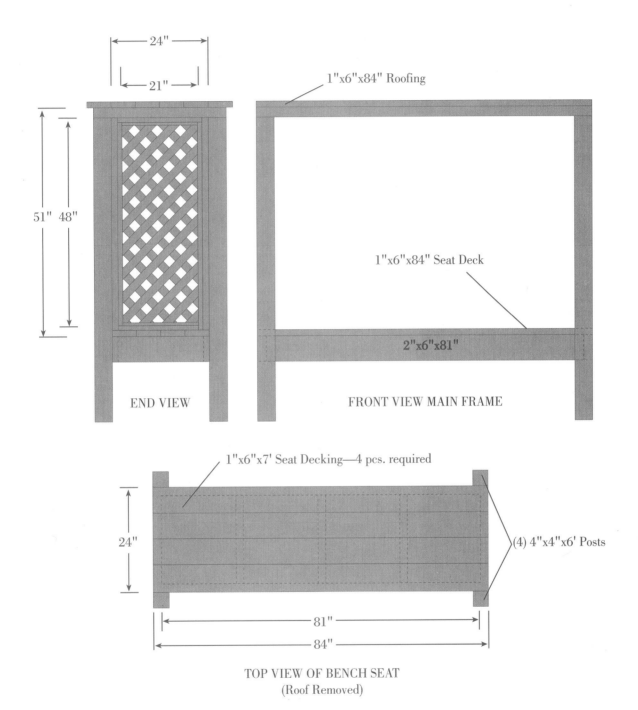

24"

21"

1"x6"x84" Roofing

51" 48"

1"x6"x84" Seat Deck

2"x6"x81"

END VIEW

FRONT VIEW MAIN FRAME

1"x6"x7' Seat Decking—4 pcs. required

24"

(4) 4"x4"x6' Posts

81"

84"

TOP VIEW OF BENCH SEAT
(Roof Removed)

The curve of a rounded arbor
presents a builder with a greater
structural challenge. This one in
Vermont is proportioned and placed
to best advantage.

STORAGE EMBRACED BY A PERGOLA

The client in Brooklyn whose back house wall I covered with lattice was also in need of a tool shed. It so happened that a wisteria limb was creeping into the rear of the yard from a neighbor's. I came up with the idea of killing two birds with one stone. I nestled a 6'x8', lattice-covered tool storage cabin within the confines of a 19'-long pergola, thereby providing a hiding place for equipment and sturdy support for the wisteria that will eventually climb over it.

The upper assemblage is of classic pergola form: two support beams spanned by notched cross members, egg-crate style. If you use the round columns indicated, only five will be needed because one can be halved to make the two columns flanking the doorway. The two columns at the edges of the shed need to have a quarter-round pie wedge cut out of each to accommodate the corners of the shed. A much easier solution would be to use square, rather than round, columns.

Be sure to slope the roof of the shed slightly, as indicated, to allow for thorough drain off of rainwater.

The toolshed was enclosed within a pergola containing eight support columns, which would eventually support the wisteria's mature growth. The outside of the toolshed was appliquéd with lattice to enhance the effect.

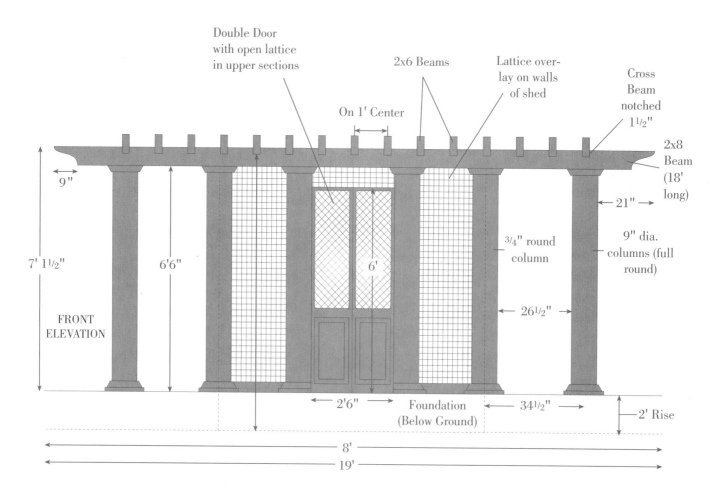

Double Door with open lattice in upper sections

2x6 Beams

Lattice overlay on walls of shed

Cross Beam notched 1½"

On 1' Center

2x8 Beam (18' long)

9"

21"

¾" round column

9" dia. columns (full round)

7' 1½"

6'6"

6'

26½"

FRONT ELEVATION

2'6"

Foundation (Below Ground)

34½"

2' Rise

8'

19'

PERGOLA TOOL SHED

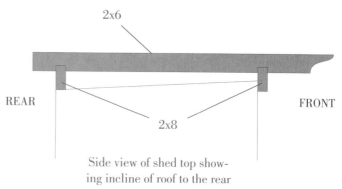

2x6

REAR

2x8

FRONT

Side view of shed top showing incline of roof to the rear

The same clients who asked me to cover the facade of their building also asked me to design a small (8'x8') toolshed at the rear end of their garden.

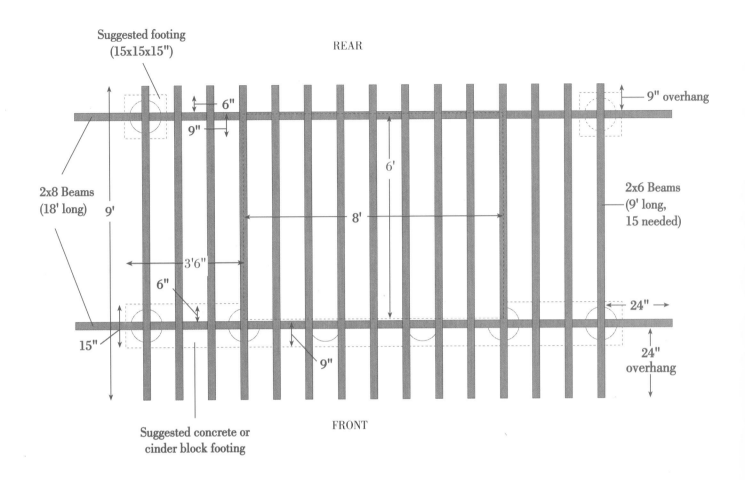

Suggested footing
(15x15x15")

REAR

9" overhang

6"

9"

6'

2x8 Beams
(18' long)

9'

8'

2x6 Beams
(9' long,
15 needed)

3'6"

6"

6'

15"

9"

24"

24"
overhang

Suggested concrete or
cinder block footing

FRONT

MATERIALS REQUIRED

LUMBER:

(15) 9 ft. lengths of 2 x 6
(2) 18 ft. lengths of 2 x 8
(2) 8 ft. lengths of 1 x 3
(8) sheets of 4 x 8 ft. lattice
(5) columns—6'6" tall, 9" diameter (full
     round)
(6) standard cinder blocks

HARDWARE:

10 penny galvanized nails
4 penny galvanized nails
4 exterior (brass) hinges

THE VIEW FROM HERE IS JUST FINE

Whether situated alongside a tennis court or a swimming pool, this structure was conceived as a viewing pavilion to shield spectators from the sun. The basic conformation is a classic pergola, with sides filled in with lattice panels, arches, and elliptical windows (which I favor over round). Measuring fourteen feet square, three sides are identical, with an equal amount of enclosure, while the fourth is open to allow as much view as possible with minimal obstruction.

The entire structure is supported by four square, latticed columns, the construction of which is indicated in the project that follows. The lattice between the columns consists of modular panels, as indicated in the diagram. The keystones are cut from $1/2$" marine-grade plywood, and the arches and windows are fabricated according to the indications suggested for a curved arbor, briefly described on page 119.

A 14'x14' tennis court pavilion provides necessary shade and comfort for spectators and players alike.

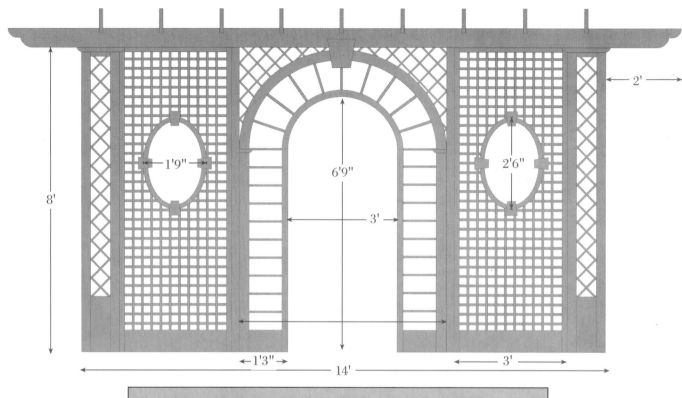

WEST, NORTH, & EAST FRONTS OF LATTICED PAVILION

The roof is of traditional pergola parameters—nine notched beams resting on two support members. If you are so inclined, this particular structure lends itself well to a clever optional add-on. Troughs measuring 12"x12", with holes punched in the bottom for drainage, may be built of plywood and placed around the perimeter of the roof. Set container plants into the troughs, and if they happen to be of the trailing variety, such as cascading geraniums, they will make quite a show of bloom, lending the illusion that a vining plant is topping off the pavilion with an explosion of leaves and flowers.

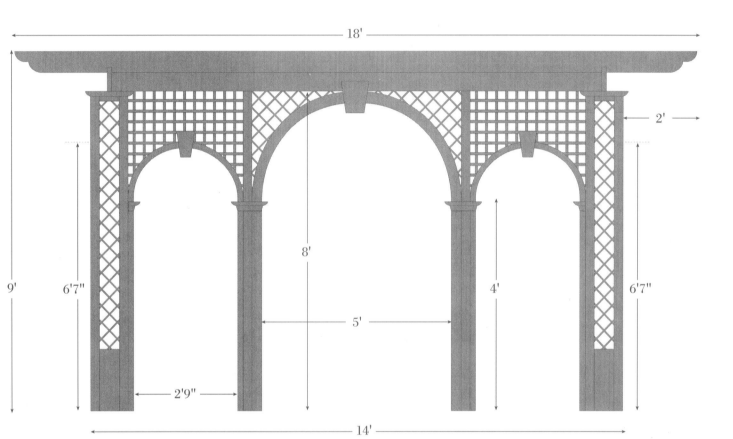

SOUTH FRONT OF LATTICED PAVILION

MATERIALS REQUIRED

LUMBER:

(9) 14 ft. lengths of 2 x 6
(2) 18 ft. lengths of 2 x 6
(2) 10 ft. lengths of 1 x 6
(2) sheets of marine plywood
(9) sheets of treated lattice
For South Front of Latticed Pavilion (above):
(3) additional sheets of treated lattice

HARDWARE:

10 penny (10d) nails
4 penny (4d) nails

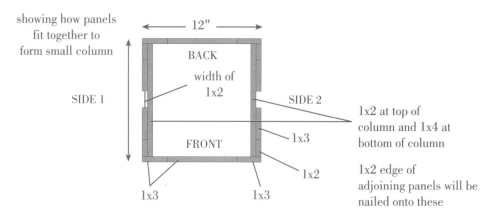

TOP VIEW

showing how panels
fit together to
form small column

BACK

width of
1x2

SIDE 1

SIDE 2

12"

FRONT

1x3

1x2

1x3   1x3

1x2 at top of
column and 1x4 at
bottom of column

1x2 edge of
adjoining panels will be
nailed onto these

SMALL COLUMN FOR LATTICED PAVILION

MATERIALS REQUIRED:

LUMBER:

(1) 10 ft. length of $\frac{1}{2}$-round
(1) 10 ft. length of 1x8
(2) sheets of treated lattice

For small columns:
(4) 10 ft. lengths of 1x3
(4) 10 ft. lengths of 1x2

Side of Circle Panels
(most lumber included
in above lists):
(2) 10 ft. lengths of 1x2

HARDWARE:

4 penny (4d) nails
1 $\frac{5}{8}$ inch exterior decking screws

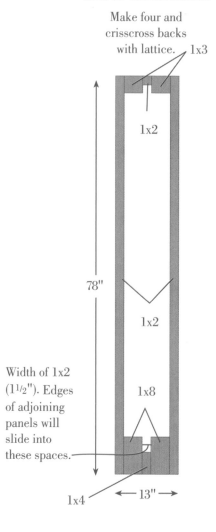

SIDE OF CIRCLE PANELS

Make four and
crisscross backs
with lattice.

1x3

1x2

78"

1x2

Width of 1x2
(1$\frac{1}{2}$"). Edges
of adjoining
panels will
slide into
these spaces.

1x8

1x4

13"

Square and rectangular lattice columns have been

mainstays in most of my designs.

They have enormous versatility, able to take the place

of a round column to support whatever

needs supporting. On these two pages are

plans for the small columns of the latticed pavilion (the same small

columns used for the Flower Show fence shown on page 139).

Plans for large columns are on page 138.

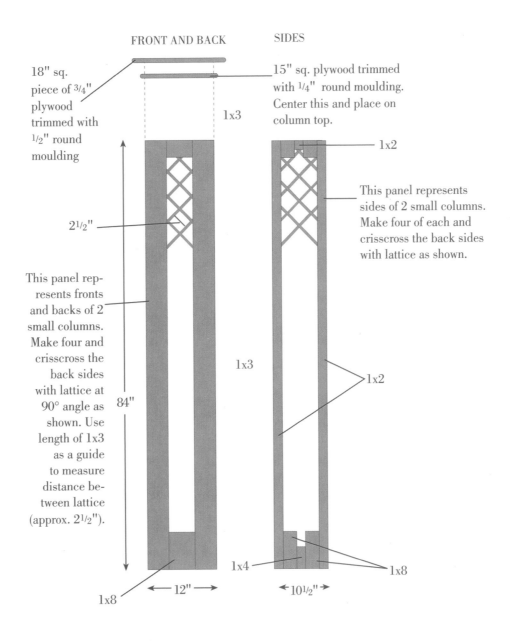

FRONT AND BACK   SIDES

18" sq. piece of ³/₄" plywood trimmed with ¹/₂" round moulding

15" sq. plywood trimmed with ¹/₄" round moulding. Center this and place on column top.

1x3

1x2

2¹/₂"

This panel represents sides of 2 small columns. Make four of each and crisscross the back sides with lattice as shown.

This panel represents fronts and backs of 2 small columns. Make four and crisscross the back sides with lattice at 90° angle as shown. Use length of 1x3 as a guide to measure distance between lattice (approx. 2¹/₂").

84"

1x3

1x2

1x8

1x4

1x8

12"

10¹/₂"

A Fence with Opportunity

The original version of this 52'-long fence made its debut at the 1989 New York Flower Show and was given an award for original design by the Pennsylvania Horticultural Society. That fence was entirely symmetrical, with the main moon gate at its center, and it now sits at C. Z. Guest's property on Long Island. Illustrated here is an adaptation dictated by the special requirements of another site, the backyard of a restored Victorian house in New Jersey. I tell you this to exemplify the absolute versatility of this particular design. Its various modules may be arranged in whatever order you prefer or your site requires.

I wish you the greatest success and joy with all your latticework adventures, however humble or grand they may be.

This fence in Closter, New Jersey, is of nearly identical design and color to the Flower Show fence. Certain adaptations from the original were unavoidable to accommodate a driveway for heavy equipment. The main gate was shifted to the end of the construction, and a smaller gate at the center was created for people passage.

SMALL GATE

Cut 3 half circles from ³/₄" marine plywood. Then cut each to form overhead arbor and top of gate, as shown.

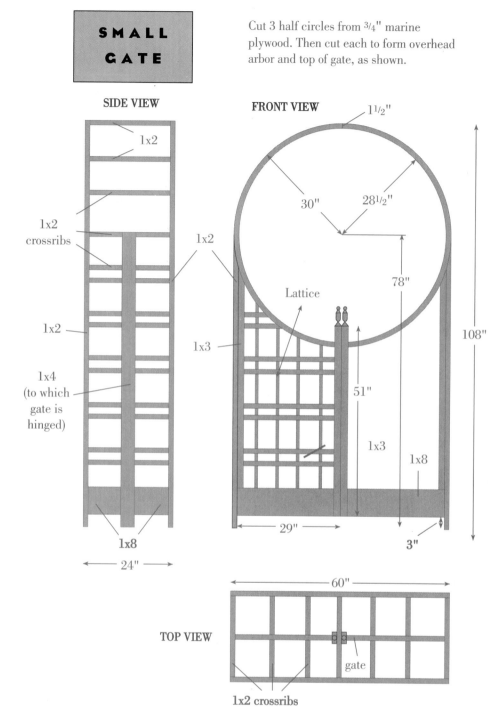

SIDE VIEW

1x2

1x2 crossribs

1x2

1x4 (to which gate is hinged)

1x8

24"

FRONT VIEW

1¹/₂"

30"   28¹/₂"

1x2

Lattice

1x3

78"

51"

1x3   1x8

29"   3"

108"

TOP VIEW

60"

gate

1x2 crossribs

MATERIALS REQUIRED:
(for small gate)

LUMBER:

(16) 8 ft. lengths of 1 x 2
(4) 10 ft. lengths of 1 x 2
(1) 10 ft. length of 1 x 8
(4) 10 ft. lengths of 1 x 3
(4) sheets of ³/₄-inch marine plywood
(2) sheets of treated lattice

HARDWARE:

4d, 8d galvanized finishing nails
2 inch galvanized screws
4 exterior (brass) gate hinges
1 gate latch

MATERIALS REQUIRED:
(for large gate)

LUMBER:

(1) 8 ft. length of 1 x 8
(8) 8 ft. lengths of 1 x 4
(2) 8 ft. length of 1 x 3
(4) 2 ¹/₄-inch round wooden door pulls
(4) sheets ³/₄-inch marine plywood
(5) sheets treated lattice

HARDWARE:

4d, 8d, 10d galvanized finishing nails
Galvanized screws as needed
6 exterior gate hinges
1 large gate latch

LARGE GATE

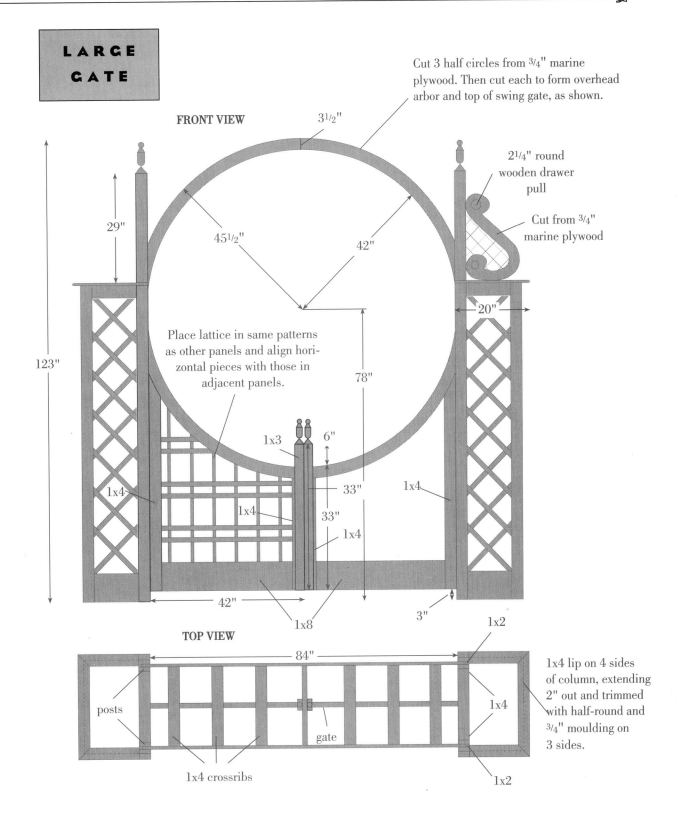

FRONT VIEW

Cut 3 half circles from ³/₄" marine plywood. Then cut each to form overhead arbor and top of swing gate, as shown.

3¹/₂"

2¹/₄" round wooden drawer pull

Cut from ³/₄" marine plywood

29"

45¹/₂"

42"

20"

123"

Place lattice in same patterns as other panels and align horizontal pieces with those in adjacent panels.

78"

1x4

1x3

6"

1x4

33"

1x4

33"

1x4

1x4

42"

3"

1x8

TOP VIEW

84"

1x2

1x4 lip on 4 sides of column, extending 2" out and trimmed with half-round and ³/₄" moulding on 3 sides.

posts

1x4

gate

1x4 crossribs

1x2

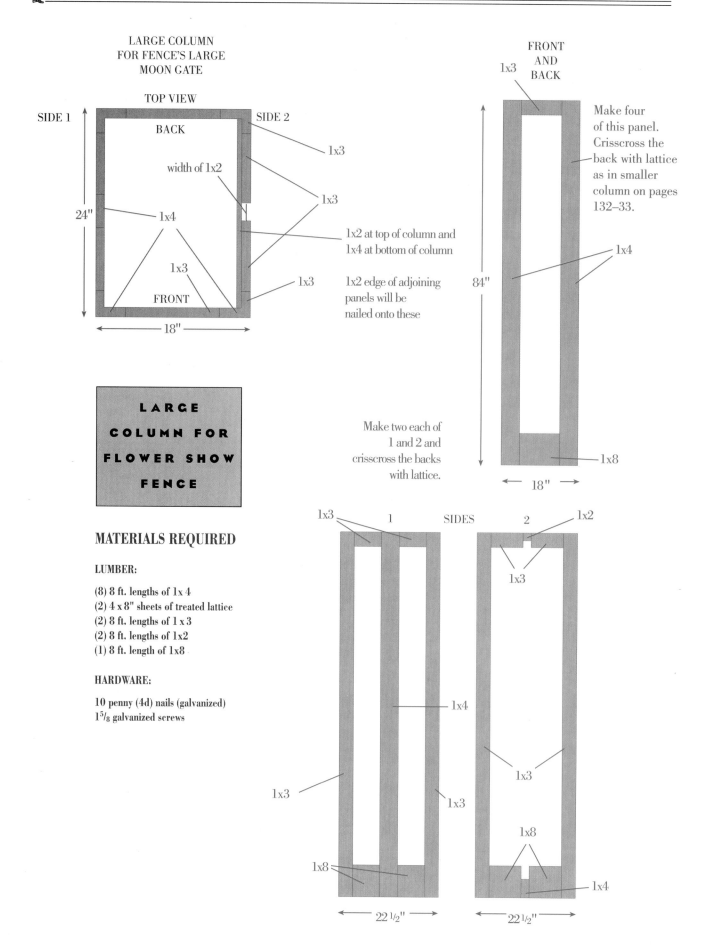

LARGE COLUMN
FOR FENCE'S LARGE
MOON GATE

TOP VIEW

SIDE 1

BACK

SIDE 2

1x3

width of 1x2

1x3

24"

1x4

1x2 at top of column and
1x4 at bottom of column

1x3

1x3

1x2 edge of adjoining
panels will be
nailed onto these

FRONT

18"

FRONT
AND
BACK

1x3

Make four
of this panel.
Crisscross the
back with lattice
as in smaller
column on pages
132–33.

1x4

84"

1x8

18"

Make two each of
1 and 2 and
crisscross the backs
with lattice.

1x3   1   SIDES   2   1x2

1x3

LARGE
COLUMN FOR
FLOWER SHOW
FENCE

1x4

1x3

MATERIALS REQUIRED

LUMBER:

(8) 8 ft. lengths of 1x 4
(2) 4 x 8" sheets of treated lattice
(2) 8 ft. lengths of 1 x 3
(2) 8 ft. lengths of 1x2
(1) 8 ft. length of 1x8

HARDWARE:

10 penny (4d) nails (galvanized)
1⅝ galvanized screws

1x3

1x3

1x8

1x3

1x8

1x8

1x4

22 ½"

22 ½"

Concrete footings indicated by dotted lines

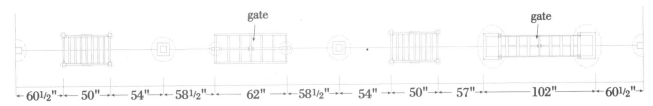

← 60½" → ← 50" → ← 54" → ← 58½" → ← 62" → ← 58½" → ← 54" → ← 50" → ← 57" → ← 102" → ← 60½" →

56'

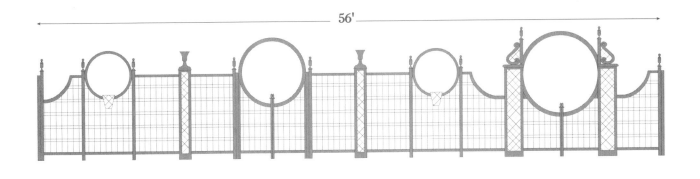

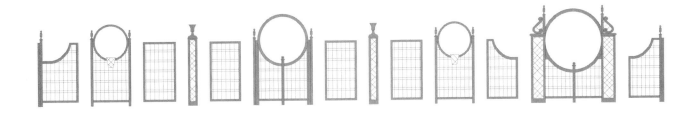

FLOWER SHOW FENCE

The 100 Best Vines

Vines are to the garden architect as fabrics are to the interior designer. They are the most fluid of plants, and whether relied on to hide an unsightly view or to enhance a glorious one, perhaps framed by an arbor or pergola, vines are also an important source of verticality, an integral facet of garden design that is often overlooked.

True vines—unlike shrubs of such sprawling habit that they are treated as vines—are capable of taking on the shape of whatever they are trained on or encouraged to climb over. The photographs selected for this chapter suggest numerous ways to enjoy vines in all kinds of gardens, large and small, even those dedicated to growing vegetables and herbs.

Charles Darwin, having observed how some plants move themselves about, wrote *The Movements and Habits of Plants*. Precisely how a vine climbs is something the gardener must know to intelligently select the right vine for the right application.

Young vines in general need reasonably slender canes or round stakes on which to become established. Some with tendrils—the

sweet pea is a prime example— need twigs set at the time of planting, so that the very first delicate tendrils can catch hold and start upward, becoming larger and stronger as height is gained. Vines with rootlike holdfasts, tendril-tip stick-tight discs, or aerial rootlets are best suited to rough surfaces such as brick, rock, stone, or masonry, and less suited to wood or aluminum siding.

Clambering and scandent plants often achieve vine status only in response to consistent and regular tying in of new growth to a trellis or other means of support (a chain-link fence in some situations). Spine- and thorn-climbers such as lemon cactus (*Pereskia*) and certain exuberant roses naturally climb ever upward at the expense of neighboring plants. The gardener intent on having them obey the configurations of a lattice or other garden structure, even one as simple as a tepee, must also be prepared to restrain errant canes, to coax and tie them according to the desired shape.

Setting a vine so as to encourage its cohabitation with a tree invites everything from spectacular results to disaster. Some vines successfully treated this way include actinidia, aristolochia, clematis, euonymus,

The terms used here focus on twining stems, coiling or disc-tipped tendrils, and aerial roots or rootlike holdfasts, but there are other means, some of them highly individual adaptations, by which vines or vinelike plants become airborne. These can be described variously as:

Stem-twining

Tendril-twining

Scandent/climbing

Tendril-climbing

Clambering

Coiled leaf-stalk

Half-twisting

Aerial rootlet climbers

Disc-tipped tendrils

Root-like holdfasts

Spine

Thorn

hedera, hydrangea, parthenocissus, vitis, and wisteria. Climbing and rambling roses, 'Lady Banks,' for example, sometimes twine around and up into large deciduous trees and may in time succeed the host.

LEFT, Calystegia *graces this short expanse of steps with a burst of color when in bloom.*

THE 100 BEST VINES

NOTE: *The plant names in this collection are generally consistent with* The New Royal Horticultural Society Dictionary Index of Garden Plants, *edited by Mark Griffiths (Timber Press, Inc., 1994). Sometimes, for the sake of giving more specific information in as few words as possible, there may be slightly different treatments for the individual genus or plant entries.*

ACTINIDIA

ACTINIDIA

Actinidia arguta. Tara vine, bower actinidia. Bold, to 50 feet, hardy to northern New England. Flowers small, fragrant; fruit yellow-green, edible.

A. deliciosa (A. chinensis). Chinese gooseberry, Yangtao. Hardy where citrus are grown. Specimen vine. Young branches handsomely red-hairy. Commercial kiwi production requires the presence of male and female cultivars.

A. kolomikta. Male vine's green leaves marked white and rose-pink early in the season. Flowers small, fragrant; fruit smooth-skinned, delectable eaten out of hand.

A. polygama. Silver vine. Male plant's young leaves have silvery coloring. Cats are attracted to this vine. Edible yellow fruit.

HABIT: Twining. **HEIGHT:** 20 to 50 feet. **FOLIAGE:** Deciduous; bold, green, sometimes variegated. **FLOWERS:** Male and female appear on separate plants; small, white. **FRAGRANCE:** Sweet. **FRUIT:** Variously edible; also varying in size and color: green, yellow, red-brown, brown, or purple. **SEASON:** Active primarily spring to fall. **WHEN TO PLANT:** Set transplants when available. Most are cold-hardy to Zone 4 (but *A. deliciosa* Zone 7); heat-tolerant to Zone 8; Zone 9 in arid regions. **LIGHT:** Full sun to part shade. **SOIL:** Well-drained, moist. **FERTILIZER:** Timed-release with micronutrients at the beginning of the growing season; side-dress in winter with well-rotted compost. **TRAINING:** Useful for quick cover, for shade, as a screen or space divider. Root restriction if grown in a large container can result in a more compact but vigorous plant, ideal for a rooftop or terrace garden.

ADLUMIA

Adlumia fungosa. Climbing fumitory, mountain fringe, Allegheny vine.

HABIT: Twining. **HEIGHT:** Tends to low bushiness in the first season, grows 15 to 25 feet and flowers the next summer, and dies by winter; a true biennial. **FOLIAGE:** Lacy, fernlike. **FLOWERS:** Resemble *Dicentra* (bleeding-heart), white to pale pink. **SEASON:** Summer. **WHEN TO PLANT:** Set transplants when available. Sow seeds in spring for flowers the next year. Cold-hardy to Zone 3, heat-tolerant to Zone 8. **LIGHT:** Half sunny to half shady. **SOIL:** Humusy, well-drained, moist. **FERTILIZER:** Side-dress fall to winter with well-rotted compost. **TRAINING:** Suited to consorting with large rocks or scrambling up trees in a semi-wild garden.

AGAPETES

Agapetes serpens.

HABIT: Scandent/climbing. **HEIGHT:** 5 to 10 feet. **FOLIAGE:** Subtropical evergreen. Small, lance-shaped leaves, resembling dwarf myrtle (*Myrtus*). **FLOWERS:** Pendent, narrow (tubular) bells, up to 1 inch long; cherry red. **SEASON:** Spring. **WHEN TO PLANT:** Set transplants when available, in the ground in Zones 9 to 10 or warmer; elsewhere, manage as container plants and keep outdoors during warm weather. **LIGHT:** Full sun to part shade. **SOIL:** Loam-based, humusy, well-drained, moist; slightly drier in fall and winter. **FERTILIZER:** Timed-release with micronutrients at the beginning of the growing season. **TRAINING:** Grown primarily for flowers; suited to espalier on fence, trellis, or wall; also for tepee as specimen accent.

AKEBIA

Akebia quinata. Five-leaf akebia. Chocolate vine.

A. trifoliata. Three-leaf akebia.

HABIT: Twining. **HEIGHT:** Rapid growth; in a single season, as much as 15 to 20 feet, but not more than 30 feet at maturity. **FOLIAGE:** Finger-shaped leaves in 3s or 5s, depending on species. *A. quinata,* evergreen in milder climates;

ALLAMANDA

A. trifoliata, deciduous. **FLOWERS:** *A. quinata,* chocolate-maroon, in spring; *A. trifoliata,* purple, in summer. **FRAGRANCE:** *A. quinata,* spice-scented. **FRUIT:** Grayish-purple, 3 to 5 inches long, and edible in *A. quinata,* but seldom formed in cultivation; violet-colored in *A. trifoliata.* **SEASON:** All-year interest. **WHEN TO PLANT:** Set transplants when available. Cold-hardy to Zone 5; heat-tolerant to Zones 8 to 9. **LIGHT:** Sunny to shady; one of the best vines for growing in shade. **SOIL:** Humusy, well-drained, moist. **FERTILIZER:** Timed-release with micronutrients at the beginning of the growing season; side-dress fall to winter with well-rotted compost. **TRAINING:** Adapted to ground cover; good on lattice structures and wire fences, or clothing a shaded wall. Combine *A. quinata* with *Clematis macropetala* 'Markham's Pink.' To rejuvenate, can be cut to the ground in spring. Also, if trained on a support, all but three or four basal shoots can be removed; the result will be more a delicate tracery than a leafy mass.

ALLAMANDA

Allamanda blanchetii (A. violacea). Purple allamanda.

A. cathartica. Golden-trumpet allamanda.

A. schottii (A. neriifolia). Bush allamanda.

HABIT: Clambering shrubs trying to be vines, or vice versa. **HEIGHT:** 10 feet tall and as wide. **FOLIAGE:** Evergreen, glossy, medium to large leaves. **FLOWERS:** Trumpets in brilliant colors. **SEASON:** Summer to fall. **WHEN TO PLANT:** Set transplants when available. Suited to container culture only, in Zone 8 and colder. Often bedded-out for summer in all zones where temperatures range from 60° to 90°F or warmer with high humidity. Containerized allamandas should be moved to a frost-free holding area, cut back, and kept on the dry side for the duration of cold weather. **LIGHT:** Sun to half-sun while in active growth. **SOIL:** Humusy, well-drained, moist (can be kept on the dry side in winter). **FERTILIZER:** Timed-release with micronutrients at the beginning of the growing season. **TRAINING:** Strong young shoots are pliable enough for training around posts and pillars, or in an upward spiral around a tepee. The plants can also be cut back several times early in the season, so that a more rounded shrub habit is achieved.

AMPELOPSIS

Ampelopsis aconitifolia. Monkshood vine. Leaves lacy, 5-lobed. Flowers inconspicuous. Berries bluish in early fall, mature to orange and yellow.

A. arborea. Pepper vine. Leaves semi-evergreen, deeply cut, lacy, almost fernlike, with reddish-bronze cast. Grows rapidly, to 15 feet the first year.

A. brevipedunculata. Amur or porcelain ampelopsis, turquoise berry. Leaves large, spring green; 'Elegans' leaves

are smaller, variegated pinkish white when young. Berries pea-sized, in showy color combinations as individuals change from acid green to lavender and purple, or aquamarine, turquoise, and steel blue, to ultramarine—sometimes all colors appearing at once on the same vine or even in the same cluster.

AMPELOPSIS

A. cordata. Heart-leaf ampelopsis. Big and strong; large leaves; berries clear blue.

A. humulifolia. Hop ampelopsis. Leaves grape-shaped, white reverses; fruits yellow to blue.

HABIT: Tendril-climbing. **HEIGHT:** 15 to 30 feet. Control by thinning yearly in early spring. **SEASON:** Foliage, spring to fall; berries in fall; vinewood and twig tracery in winter. **WHEN TO PLANT:** Set transplants when available, usually spring; sometimes sold containerized and wrapped around a stake. Widely cold- and heat-tolerant, Zones 4–5 through Zones 9–10. **LIGHT:** Full sun to part shade. **SOIL:** Well-drained, moist to on the dry side. **FERTILIZER:** Timed-release with micronutrients at planting time. Thereafter, side-dress fall to winter with compost. **TRAINING:** Fast cover for walls, arbors, fences, trellises.

ANREDERA

Anredera cordifolia (Boussingaultia baselloides). Madeira vine, mignonette vine.

HABIT: Tendril-twining. **HEIGHT:** To 20 feet. **FOLIAGE:** Evergreen if not subjected to freezing; leaves heart-shaped, to 3 inches long. **FLOWERS:** Small, in showy spikelike clusters; white. **FRAGRANCE:** Sweet. **FRUIT:** None. Small tubercles that appear in the leaf axils toward the end of the growing season can be harvested, wintered in a warm place, then planted at the beginning of the next growing season as though they were seeds. **SEASON:** All year in Zone 9 and warmer. Warm weather until fall frost in Zones 3–8. **WHEN TO PLANT:** Set roots or tubercles (see under Fruit) at the beginning of the growing season. Cold-hardy to Zone 9 and warmer; elsewhere, dig the roots and store them with some of the newly formed tubercles in a warm place until planting time the next year. **LIGHT:** Full sun to part shade. **SOIL:** Well-drained, moist, sandy loam. **FERTILIZER:** Timed-release with micronutrients at planting time or at the beginning of the growing season. **TRAINING:** Quick screening on a wire fence or trellis; useful to hide an eyesore.

ANTIGONON

Antigonon leptopus. Coral vine, corallita, pink vine, confederate vine, Rosa de Montana, mountain rose, love's chain, Queen Anne's wreath.

HABIT: Tendril-climbing. **HEIGHT:** 20 to 40 feet. **FOLIAGE:** Evergreen, heart-shaped, crinkly-textured. **FLOWERS:** In long, trailing sprays; individually small; typical for a member of the buckwheat family; altogether showy: bright pink in the species, white in the variety 'Alba.' **SEASON:** Variously spring, summer, or fall; flowers most prodigiously with full sun, lean soil, hot days and cool nights. **WHEN TO PLANT:** Set transplants when available. Cold- and heat-tolerant

ANTIGONON

Zones 8 to 10. May be containerized in Zone 7 and colder, trained on a trellis, and cut back sharply at the end of the season. If kept above freezing through the winter, new shoots will sprout from the roots at the beginning of the next warm season. **LIGHT:** Full sun. The vines will grow in half shade but will flower poorly. **SOIL:** Sandy loam, well-drained, evenly moist to on the dry side. **FERTILIZER:** Timed-release with micronutrients at planting time or in the spring. **TRAINING:** Popular in the South for porches and balconies, and as cover for fences, walls, and even debris. Grows readily from seeds or cuttings. Freshly opened flower sprays last well in bouquets.

ARAUJIA

Araujia sericofera. Cruel vine.

HABIT: Stem-twining. **HEIGHT:** To 20 feet. **FOLIAGE:** Evergreen, oval-oblong leaves, 2 to 4 inches long. **FLOWERS:** Small, white. **FRAGRANCE:** Lightly sweet to pungent. **SEASON:** Foliage, spring to fall; flowers, late summer to fall. **WHEN TO PLANT:** Set transplants when available. Zones 3–9 suitable for container culture only; cold-hardy to Zone 10. **LIGHT:** Full to half sun. **SOIL:** Sandy loam, evenly moist except on the dry side during cooler winter temperatures. **FERTILIZER:** Timed-release with micronutrients at planting time or in spring.

TRAINING: Choice for a white garden. Propagate from seeds under glass in winter to spring or outdoors in spring to summer.

ARISTOLOCHIA

Aristolochia macrophylla (A. durior, A. sipho). Dutchman's pipe. To 30 feet. Leaves large, heart-shaped, to 1 foot long. Flowers yellowish-green with a U-shaped tube that flattens into a purplish-brown top. Cold-hardy Zone 4. Herbaceous perennial (dies to ground in the winter).

A. elegans. Calico flower. To 10 feet. Cold-hardy to Zone 9. Leaves kidney- or heart-shaped, 2 to 3 inches long. Flowers yellowish-green tubes 1$\frac{1}{2}$ inches long, expanding to 3 inches wide, with white markings on purplish brown.

A. grandiflora. Pelican flower.

A. tomentosa. Rooster flower.

HABIT: Stem-twining. **SEASON:** Spring to fall, or any warm, frost-free time. **WHEN TO PLANT:** Set transplants when available, usually at the beginning of a growing season. **LIGHT:** Full sun to part shade. **SOIL:** Humusy, well-drained, evenly moist. **FERTILIZER:** Timed-release with micronutrients at planting time or at the beginning of a new season. **TRAINING:** Quick, attractive cover for wire fences and all manner of arbors, trellises, pillars, and pergolas. There are temperate and tropical species native to both hemispheres.

ASARINA (MAURANDYA)

Asarina antirrhinifolia. Violet twining snapdragon.

A. barclaiana. Vigorous. Flowers showy, to 3 inches long, purple; rose and white varieties are also available.

A. erubescens. Creeping gloxinia. Tender perennial with downy leaves; flowers to 3 inches long, rose-pink.

ARISTOLOCHIA

HABIT: Coiled leafstalk climber. **HEIGHT:** 3 to 6 feet. **FOLIAGE:** Ivy-shaped. **FLOWERS:** Tubular, 5-lobed, to 3 inches. **SEASON:** Much of the year in Zone 10; elsewhere, often treated as an annual, grown from seeds or cuttings started in a warm place indoors in winter and transplanted to the garden at the beginning of summer. **WHEN TO PLANT:** Set transplants when available, usually at the beginning of a season of warm weather, outdoors or in a greenhouse. **LIGHT:** Full to half sun. **SOIL:** Humusy, well-drained, moist to on the dry side. **FERTILIZER:** Timed-release with micronutrients at planting time; also at the beginning of the growing season. **TRAINING:** Suited to covering small trellises and minor fences; ideal for container gardening, or set in a window box to adorn lattice panels placed on either side of the window.

ASPARAGUS

Asparagus asparagoides. Smilax of floristry. Grows to 20 feet.

A. falcatus. Sicklethorn asparagus. Grows to 40 feet.

HABIT: Twining. **FOLIAGE:** Evergreen, shiny, fresh. **FLOWERS:** Small, white, inconspicuous. **FRAGRANCE:** Sweet. **FRUIT:** Purple or brown berries. **SEASON:** Evergreen. **WHEN TO PLANT:** Set transplants when available. Cold- and heat-tolerant in Zones 9–10; elsewhere, grow in containers and bring to a frost-free place when temperatures drop below 40°F. Freezing, or cutting to the ground in spring, can result in a rejuvenated plant. **LIGHT:** Full sun to part shade. **SOIL:** Loam-based, well-drained, moist. **FERTILIZER:** Timed-release with micronutrients at planting time or at the beginning of a new season. **TRAINING:** For screening, train on almost any fence or trellis. Smilax can be cut freely for floral decorations.

BASELLA

Malabar spinach, Ceylon spinach

HABIT: Twining, cascading, scrambling annual. **HEIGHT:** From 3 to 25 feet. **FOLIAGE:** 2 to 6 inches, irregularly oblong, heart-shaped, to broadly ovate; glossy light to dark green, crinkly with red veins in 'Rubra' variety. *B.alba* is edible. **FLOWERS:** Inflorescences to 7 inches with white, rose, red, or purple blossoms. **FRUIT:** Varies from black, dark red to white, glossy. **SEASON:** Summer only, dies in autumn. **WHEN TO PLANT:** Start seeds indoors; set transplants after all danger of frost has passed in Zones 9 or warmer. **LIGHT:** Full sun. **SOIL:** Loam-based, humusy, well-drained, moist. **FERTILIZER:** Timed-release with micronutrients at beginning of growing season. **TRAINING:** Use to cover trellis, arbor, or wire-mesh fence, tends toward unruliness if not harvested frequently.

BEAUMONTIA

Beaumontia grandiflora. Nepal trumpet flower, Easter lily vine.

HABIT: Half-twisting stems. **HEIGHT:** 10 to 20 feet. **FOLIAGE:** Evergreen leaves, oval, dark green, to 8 inches long. **FLOWERS:** Trumpet-shaped, to 5 inches across; white. **FRAGRANCE:** Vanilla. **SEASON:** Spring to summer. **WHEN TO PLANT:** Set transplants when available. Suited to growing in the ground only in Zone 10; elsewhere, manage as a container plant that can be kept outdoors for the duration of warm weather. **LIGHT:** Full sun. **SOIL:** Loam-based, humusy, evenly moist while in active growth, on the dry side in cool winter temperatures. **FERTILIZER:** Timed-release with micronutrients at planting time; at the beginning of the growing season. **TRAINING:** Woody, strong vines, suited to training on suitably strong fences, trellises, or arbors.

BENINCASA

Benincasa hispida. Wax gourd, Chinese water melon.

HABIT: Tendril-climbing. **HEIGHT:** 15 to 25 feet. **FOLIAGE:** five-lobed leaves, rounded or kidney-shaped. **FLOWERS:** Male and female on the same plant. **FRUIT:** Melonlike, 8 to 15 inches long; edible, often preserved or used in curries. **SEASON:** Grown mostly as a hot-weather annual. **WHEN TO PLANT:** Sow seeds where they are to grow—next to a trellis, fence, or other means of support—as soon as the ground is warm and the weather settled. **LIGHT:** Full sun. **SOIL:** Loam-based, humusy, well-drained but abundantly watered. **FERTILIZER:** Timed-release with micronutrients at planting time. **TRAINING:** This native of tropical Asia grows quickly in hot summer weather and gives an exotic appearance wherever trained, especially if on an arbor or tepee so that the hanging fruits can be observed as they develop.

BERBERIDOPSIS

Berberidopsis corallina. Chile vine, coral plant.

HABIT: Stem-twining. **HEIGHT:** 10 to 15 feet. **FOLIAGE:** Leaves evergreen, heart-shaped, to 3 inches long, coarsely toothed. **FLOWERS:** Coral-red in pendant clusters. **FRUIT:** A berry. **SEASON:** Summer flowers. **WHEN TO PLANT:** Set transplants in the ground in Zone 10 only. Elsewhere, manage as a container plant and keep outdoors except when temperatures fall below 40°F. Maintain in a cool, sunny greenhouse until spring. **LIGHT:** Full to half sun. **SOIL:** Loam-based, humusy, with added sphagnum peat moss; keep evenly moist. **FERTILIZER:** Timed-release with micronutrients at the beginning of the warm season. **TRAINING:** Sprawling habit makes it a good idea to begin training this potentially glorious tropical early to develop a pleasing branch structure. Prune freely after the flowering season for compactness and generous flower production the following year.

BIGNONIA

Bignonia capreolata. Cross vine.

HABIT: Tendril-climbing. **HEIGHT:** 25 to 50 feet. **FOLIAGE:** Evergreen; two leaflets, opposite; to 6 inches long. **FLOWERS:** Tubular, to 2 inches, in clusters; yellow-red. **SEASON:** Flowers in spring; foliage all year in warmer regions, herbaceous in regions with temperatures below 20°F. **WHEN TO PLANT:** Set transplants when available, in the ground in Zone 6 and warmer. Elsewhere, this vine maintained as container plant, to be put outdoors for the duration of warm, frost-free weather. **LIGHT:** Full sun. **SOIL:** Loam-based, well-drained, moist. **FERTILIZER:** Timed-release with micronutrients at planting time, or at the beginning of a season of active growth. **TRAINING:** Suited to all kinds of garden structures, fences, pergolas, screens, around columns and posts.

BILLARDIERA

Billardiera longiflora. Blueberry.

HABIT: Stem-twining. **HEIGHT:** 15 to 30 feet. **FOLIAGE:** Evergreen. **FLOWERS:** Greenish-white to purplish. **FRUIT:** Edible; blue. A must for the blue garden. **SEASON:** Spring to fall. **WHEN TO PLANT:** Set transplants when available, in the ground in Zone 9 and warmer only . Elsewhere, manage as a container plant on a trellis, transferring outdoors during warm, frost-free weather. **LIGHT:** Full sun. **SOIL:** Loam-based, humusy, well-drained, moist. **FERTILIZER:** Timed-release with micronutrients at planting time or at the beginning of the new growing season, either late winter or spring. **TRAINING:** Prune back to main stem framework after the berries fall.

BOMAREA

Bomarea caldasii.

HABIT: Stem-twining. **HEIGHT:** 10 to 14 feet. **FOLIAGE:** Deciduous; oval leaves on twisted leaf stalks. **FLOWERS:** Resembling Peruvian lily (*Alstroemeria*), funnel-shaped, in showy, drooping clusters; red to reddish-brown with bright yellow inner segments. **SEASON:** Flowers in summer. **WHEN TO PLANT:** Set transplants when available, Zone 9 or warmer. Elsewhere, maintain as a container plant. Set initially into a medium-size or large pot and plan not to disturb the roots for several years, or until they are pushing the entire plant up out of the pot. **LIGHT:** Full sun. **SOIL:** Loam-based, humusy, well-drained, moist spring to summer, on the dry side fall to winter. **FERTILIZER:** Timed-release with micronutrients at the beginning of the active growing season late winter or spring. **TRAINING:** Suited to wires, strings, or mesh that can be used in connection with almost any trellis, fence, wall, or post.

BOUGAINVILLEA

Bougainvillea glabra. Paper flower.

HABIT: Sprawling to dwarf thorn clamberers. **HEIGHT:** 5 to 60 feet. **FOLIAGE:** Deciduous. **FLOWERS:** Small white to pale yellow trumpets in much larger bracts, which can be yellow, orange, peach, copper, white, or glowing red-magenta. **SEASON:** Everblooming in Zone 10, summer or winter. Zone 9 and colder, move indoors any time frost is likely. **WHEN TO PLANT:** Set transplants when available; containerize for indoor/outdoor treatment in Zone 9 and colder. **LIGHT:** Sunny. **SOIL:** Well-drained, moist to on the dry side. **FERTILIZER:** Potash-rich, such as 12-12-17, preferably timed-release with micronutrients, at the beginning of a growing season. **TRAINING:** Bougainvillea climbs by means of needle-sharp spines. Carefully tie branches to a trellis, fence, tepee, or other means of support. After an old branch has bloomed profusely, it should be removed as low down on the plant as possible to stimulate strong new basal shoots that will mature and bloom in the future. Branches that arch over or are tied horizontally flower more profusely.

CALYSTEGIA

Calystegia hederacea.(Convolvulus japonicus). Japanese bindweed.

HABIT: Twining stems. **HEIGHT:** To 15 feet. **FOLIAGE:** Narrow arrowheads, to 3 inches long. **FLOWERS:** Funnelform, to 2 inches, or rose, double in the cultivar 'Flore Pleno.' ("California rose" in the nursery trade.) **SEASON:** Summer to fall flowers. **WHEN TO PLANT:** Set transplants when available. **LIGHT:** Half to full sun. **SOIL:** Loam-based, well-drained, moist. **FERTILIZER:** Timed-release with micronutrients at planting time, or at the beginning of a new season. **TRAINING:** Recommended for covering banks and fences, for tepees or any kind of lattice.

BOUGAINVILLEA

CAMPSIS

Campsis grandiflora. Chinese trumpet creeper.

C. radicans. Trumpet vine.

C. x *tagliabuana* (orange and scarlet). *'Mme Galen'* (dark-veined apricot).

HABIT: Aerial rootlet-climbers. **HEIGHT:** *C. grandiflora,* to 20 feet; *C. radicans,* 30 to 40 feet; *C.* x *tagliabuana,* 10 to 20 feet. **FOLIAGE:** Deciduous; leaves odd-pinnate, 6 to 8 inches long. **FLOWERS:** Funnel-shaped, to 3 inches long, in showy clusters; scarlet, dark orange, apricot. **SEASON:** Flowers mid-summer to early fall; leaves spring until frost. **WHEN TO PLANT:** Set transplants when available, in the ground in almost any zone. Campsis vines may also be containerized for all kinds of terrace and roof gardens. **LIGHT:** Full sun. **SOIL:** Loam-based, well-drained, moist. **FERTILIZER:** Timed-release with micronutrients at planting time; also at the beginning of each new growing season. **TRAINING:** Suited to covering brick, stone, and other masonry walls, also tree trunks. Not recommended for wood walls or other wood structures. The vines can become very top-heavy. Some campsis travel by underground runners that may pop up a great distance from the source and can even become invasive unless rigorously dug and chopped out.

CANARINA

Canarina canariensis syn. *C. campanula.* Canary Island bellflower.

HABIT: Scrambling climber; herbaceous, from a tuberous root. **HEIGHT:** 5 to 10 feet. **FOLIAGE:** Leaves oval to lance-shaped, lobed, to 3 inches long. **FLOWERS:** Bell-like, to 2 inches long; yellow with reddish or purplish lines. **SEASON:** Late fall to spring. **WHEN TO PLANT:** Set transplants when available, in the ground in Zone 9 and warmer; elsewhere, maintain in a container that

CAMPSIS

CLEMATIS

CISSUS

can be brought indoors during freezing weather. **LIGHT:** Full to half sun. **SOIL:** Loam-based, well-drained, moist while in active growth, on the dry side at other times. **FERTILIZER:** Timed-release with micronutrients at the beginning of a new growing season. **TRAINING:** A small, elegant flowering vine suited to training on lattice or wire where it can be seen at close range.

CELASTRUS

Celastrus loeseneri. Chinese bittersweet.

C. orbiculatus. Oriental bittersweet, staff vine.

C. scandens. American bittersweet, staff tree.

HABIT: Twining. **HEIGHT:** Chinese bittersweet, to 20 feet; Oriental bittersweet, to 40 feet; American bittersweet, to 25 feet. **FOLIAGE:** Deciduous; leaves ovate, obovate to elliptic, 3 to 4 inches long. **FLOWERS:** Cymes, racemes, or panicles 2 to 4 inches long; greenish, yellowish, or white. **FRUIT:** Yellow to orange enclosed in a colorful aril— yellow, orange, crimson, or vermilion when ripe. Most celastrus plants bear flowers of a single sex; plant several vines in the same vicinity to ensure pollination. **SEASON:** Fall for fruit. **WHEN TO PLANT:** Set transplants when available, to Zone 4 for American bittersweet, to Zone 7 for the others; heat tolerance through Zone 8. **LIGHT:** Full sun. **SOIL:** Well-drained, moist. **FERTILIZER:** Timed-release with micronutrients at planting time or at the beginning of a growing season. **TRAINING:** Excellent cover for banks, arbors, or trellises. Prune old wood in early spring to maintain control.

CISSUS

Cissus adenopodus. Pink cissus. Leaves three-part, leaflets elliptic to 6 inches long, olive-green with purplish-red hairs.

C. antarctica. Kangaroo vine. Leaves ovate to oblong, 3 to 4 inches long, glossy green.

C. discolor. Rex begonia vine. Leaves ovate, 4 to 7 inches long, velvety green with silver and pale pink markings.

C. rhombifolia. Grape ivy. Leaves ever-green, three-part, rhombic-ovate, 1 to 4 inches long.

HABIT: Tendril climbers. **HEIGHT:** 10 to 15 feet. **FOLIAGE:** Simple or lobed, decidu-ous or evergreen. **FLOWERS:** Small, inconspicuous, greenish-white. **FRUIT:** A dry berry, purple-black. **SEASON:** Foliage all year. **WHEN TO PLANT:** Set transplants when available, in the ground in Zone 10 or warmer only; elsewhere, maintain as container plant. **LIGHT:** Full sun to part shade. **SOIL:** Loam-based, humusy, well-drained, moist. **FERTILIZER:** Timed-release with micronutrients at the beginning of growing season. **TRAINING:** Hanging containers or on a small trellis.

CLEMATIS

Clematis.

HABIT: Leaf-stem tendril climbers. **HEIGHT:** 3 to 30 feet. **FOLIAGE:** Compound, divided, often with tendril-forming tips, usually deciduous, though there are exceptions, such as evergreen *C. armandii.* **FLOWERS:** Closed lanterns to open bells, 1 to 6 inches across. Some starry or doubled, all colors including blue. **FRAGRANCE:** Notably in *C. flammula* and *C. terniflora* (a.k.a. *C. paniculata* and *C. maximowicziana*), but fragrance is scattered throughout the genus. **FRUIT:** Silky, feathery seed heads can be beautiful in their own right. **SEASON:** Flowers primarily spring to summer to early fall. **WHEN TO PLANT:** Set transplants when available, root-stocks immediately upon receipt from nursery. Clematis needs a season to take hold. Cold- and heat-tolerant within Zones 3–9. In spring, prune back old growth from clematis species that bloom on the current season's

shoots, but only the dead or straggly growth from any species that bloom on wood formed the previous season. **LIGHT:** Sunny to half-sunny in colder zones, shady to keep its roots cool in warmer zones. **SOIL:** Well-drained, well dug, and enlivened by yearly top-dressing with well-rotted compost; add limestone as needed to afford the pre-ferred "sweet," or alkaline, soil. **FERTILIZER:** Timed-release with micronu-trients at the beginning of the growing season. Side-dress fall or winter with compost. **TRAINING:** Cover fences, arbors, trellises, or tepees.

CLERODENDRUM

Clerodendrum. Glory-bower.

HABIT: Twining stems. **HEIGHT:** 10 to 15 feet. **FOLIAGE:** Evergreen ovals or hearts to 10 inches long/wide. **FLOWERS:** In heads, to 6 inches across or more, often with bracts that remain showy long after the more ephemeral blossoms have dropped; blue, pink, rose, scarlet, white. **FRAGRANCE:** Not in *C. thomsoni-ae*, but the genus does contain numer-ous fragrant species, notably *C. fra-grans* and *C. trichotomum*. **FRUIT:** A drupe, in various colors: white, yellow, black, purple, violet, blue, dark red. **SEASON:** Variously winter, spring, sum-mer, or fall, depending on the species and the climate. **WHEN TO PLANT:** Set transplants when available. Hardiest to cold is *C. trichotomum*, Zones 6–7; the others are tropical to subtropical, Zones 8–10, or indoors/outdoors in colder zones. **LIGHT:** Sunny to half-shady. **SOIL:** Humusy, well-drained, moist; surprisingly drought-tolerant when established. **FERTILIZER:** Timed-release with micronutrients at the beginning of a warm growing season. **TRAINING:** *C. thomsoniae* (bleeding-heart vine) readily takes hold on a lattice structure or fence, or it can be impres-sively trained into a large wreath shape on a wire or grapevine form anchored upright by tying to bamboo stakes.

CLIANTHUS

Clianthus formosus. Desert pea.

C. puniceus. Glory pea, parrot's beak.

HABIT: Scrambling climber. **HEIGHT:** 4 to 6 feet. **FOLIAGE:** Pea-like, up to 29 leaflets. **FLOWERS:** Showy, to 3 inches long, several per cluster, crimson or scarlet. **FRUIT:** Smooth, silky leathery pods, 2 to 3 inches long. **SEASON:** *C. for-mosus* blooms winter, late summer;

CLERODENDRUM

C. puniceus blooms summer to late fall. **WHEN TO PLANT:** Set transplants when available in the ground in Zones 8–9 or warmer; elsewhere, maintain as con-tainer plants that can be moved to a protected place during freezing weath-er. **LIGHT:** Full sun. **SOIL:** Loam-based, well-drained, moist to on the dry side. **FERTILIZER:** Timed-release with micronu-trients at beginning of growing season. **TRAINING:** In hanging basket or as bank cover.

CLITORIA

CLYTOSTOMA

Clytostoma callistigioides. Argentine trumpet vine.

HABIT: Tendril-climbing. **HEIGHT:** 30 to 60 feet. **FOLIAGE:** Evergreen; glossy, compound with two leaflets bearing wavy margins; up to 3 inches long. **FLOWERS:** Funnel-shaped, in pairs, to 3 inches long; pale purple with yellow in the throat. **SEASON:** Flowers in spring to summer. **WHEN TO PLANT:** Set transplants when available in the ground, Zones 9-10; elsewhere, maintain as container plant. **LIGHT:** Full sun to part shade. **SOIL:** Loam-based, humusy, well-drained, moist. **FERTILIZER:** Timed-release with micronutrients at beginning of growing season. **TRAINING:** Recommended for accent or screening.

COBAEA

Cobaea scandens. Cup and saucer vine.

HABIT: Leaflet-tendril climbing. **HEIGHT:** To 25 feet. **FOLIAGE:** Four to six leaflets, to 4 inches long; evergreen in Southern gardens. **FLOWERS:** Bell-shaped, to 2 inches, violet or greenish-purple. **FRAGRANCE:** Musky-scented initially, then honey-like. **SEASON:** Late summer to fall. **WHEN TO PLANT:** Set transplants when available or start seeds indoors in a warm, bright place in late winter. Perennial in Zones 9 and warmer. **LIGHT:** Half to full sun. **SOIL:** Loam-based, humusy, well-drained, moist. **FERTILIZER:** Timed-release with micronutrients at beginning of growing season. **TRAINING:** Suitable for covering trellises or rough walls.

CODONOPSIS

Codonopsis convolvulacea (C. vinciflora). Bonnet bellflower.

HABIT: Twining climber. **HEIGHT:** 9 to 10 feet. **FOLIAGE:** Leaves lance-shaped or oval, to 3 inches long. **FLOWERS:** Bell-like, 1 to 2 inches across, violet blue. **SEASON:** Summer to fall. **WHEN TO PLANT:**

CLITORIA

Clitoria ternatea. Butterfly pea. 'Blue Sails' semidouble, deep blue.

HABIT: Twining slender stems. **HEIGHT:** 10 to 20 feet. **FOLIAGE:** Five to seven leaflets, to 4 inches long. **FLOWERS:** To 2 inches; sea blue or white. **SEASON:** Summer or until killing frost; all zones. **WHEN TO PLANT:** Soak seeds 24 to 48 hours in room-temperature water, then sow indoors at 70° to 75°F, 12 weeks before warm, frost-free weather arrives. Set out transplants when available. **LIGHT:** Sun half day or more. **SOIL:** Well-drained, moist. **FERTILIZER:** Timed-release with micronutrients at the onset of the growing season. **TRAINING:** Quick cover for lattice, trellis, arbor, chain-link fence.

Set transplants when available, cold- and heat-tolerant within Zones 5 to 9. **LIGHT:** Half to full sun. **SOIL:** Loam-based, humusy, well-drained, moist. **FERTILIZER:** Timed-release with micronutrients at beginning of season. **TRAINING:** Recommended for training on wire fences or lattice trellis.

CRYPTOSTEGIA

Cryptostegia grandiflora. Rubber vine.

HABIT: Stem-twining, woody, strong growing. **HEIGHT:** 20 to 30 feet. **FOLIACE:** Evergreen, lustrous, oblong, to 4 inches. **FLOWERS:** Funnel-shaped, to 2 inches across in terminal clusters; purplish-lilac. **SEASON:** Summer. **WHEN TO PLANT:** Set transplants when available, in the ground in Zone 9 and warmer. Elsewhere, maintain in container. **LIGHT:** Full sun to part shade. **SOIL:** Loam-based, humusy, well-drained, moist. **FERTILIZER:** Timed-release with micronutrients at beginning of the season. **TRAINING:** Specimen or dense screening; requires sturdy trellis.

CUCURBITS

Cucumis. Cucurbit.

Cucurbita. Gourd.

Lagenaria. Bottle gourd.

Luffa. Dishcloth gourd, vegetable sponge.

HABIT: Tendril-climbing. **HEIGHT:** 15 to 30 feet. **FOLIACE:** Simple, palmate, or lobed **FLOWERS:** Male flowers in racemes, female flowers solitary. **FRUIT:** Many colors, shapes; some edible, some ornamental. **SEASON:** Summer to fall. **WHEN TO PLANT:** Sow seeds where they are to grow, after ground becomes warm. **LIGHT:** Full sun. **SOIL:** Loam-based, well-drained, moist. **FERTILIZER:** Timed-release with micronutrients at beginning of season. **TRAINING:** Suited to training as a dense screen on cord, on wire against a wall, on trellis, or on a tepee framework.

CUCURBITS

DIOSCOREA

DISTICTIS

DIOSCOREA

Dioscorea batatas. Cinnamon vine.

HABIT: Stem-twining. **HEIGHT:** 6 to 40 feet. **FOLIACE:** Ovate, 2 to 3 inches long. **FLOWERS:** Small, in spikes or racemes; greenish-white. **FRAGRANCE:** Sweetly spice-scented. **SEASON:** Summer to fall. **WHEN TO PLANT:** Set transplants when available, cold- and heat-tolerant within Zones 5 to 10. Axillary tubers may be planted in spring as seeds. **LIGHT:** Full sun to part shade. **SOIL:** Loam-based, well-drained, moist. **FERTILIZER:** Timed-release with micronutrients at beginning of season. **TRAINING:** Used mainly as screens.

DIPLOCYCLOS

Diplocyclos palmatus. (Bryonopsis laciniosa). Marble vine.

HABIT: Tendril-climbing. **HEIGHT:** 10 to 15 feet. **FOLIACE:** Deeply three- to five-lobed. **FLOWERS:** Small, in clusters; greenish. **FRUIT:** Size of a marble, green or red, striped with white. **SEASON:** Summer to fall. **WHEN TO PLANT:** Sow seeds where they are to grow, after ground becomes warm in Zone 10 or warmer; treated as an annual in most gardens. **LIGHT:** Full sun. **SOIL:** Loam-based, well-drained, moist. **FERTILIZER:** Timed-release with micronutrients at beginning of season. **TRAINING:** For quick shade or screen.

DISTICTIS

Distictis lactiflora. Vanilla trumpet vine.

HABIT: Tendril climber. **HEIGHT:** 15 to 25 feet. **FOLIACE:** Evergreen, in threes, center leaflet with twining tendril. **FLOWERS:** In clusters, each to 3 inches long, purple, fading to lavender and white. **FRAGRANCE:** Vanilla-scented. **SEASON:** Summer-fall. **WHEN TO PLANT:** Set transplants when available, in the ground in Zones 9 or warmer. Elsewhere, maintain as container specimen. **LIGHT:** Part sun to part shade.

EPIPREMNUM

SOIL: Loam-based, humusy, well-drained, moist. **FERTILIZER:** Timed-release with micronutrients at beginning of season. **TRAINING:** Light screening for trellises, fences, arbors, and other structures.

ECCREMOCARPUS

Eccremocarpus scaber. Glory flower.

HABIT: Tendril climber. **HEIGHT:** 10 to 12 feet. **FOLIAGE:** Twice pinnate. **FLOWERS:** To 1 inch long in racemes to 6 inches; orange-red. **SEASON:** Summer to fall. **WHEN TO PLANT:** Sow seeds indoors in a warm, bright place in late winter; transplant to the garden when danger of frost has passed; take care not to disturb the roots. **LIGHT:** Full to half sun. **SOIL:** Loam-based, well-drained, moist, preferably neutral to slightly alkaline pH. **FERTILIZER:** Timed-release with micronutrients at beginning of the season. **TRAINING:** For fence, trellis, or lattice structures.

EPIPREMNUM

Pothos ivy, devil's ivy (previous genus: Scindapsus).

HABIT: Adhesive roots along stems of lianes with larger leaves forming as it climbs into adult phase. **HEIGHT:** To 90 feet or more in moist tropical setting. **FOLIAGE:** Tropical evergreen lianes with juvenile and adult phases; leaves entire to pinnate, occasionally perforated in adult phase, tough but smooth and pliable, from 3 inches in juvenile to 2 feet in adult phase. Color varies from solid medium green to yellow or white variegation as in *E. aureum.* **FLOWERS:** Peduncle (flower stalk) appears short and solitary, cymbiform (boat-like with central spine) spathe to 1 1/2 inches does not form a tube, its yellow to green or purple shroud contains a short, stout spadix. **FRUIT:** Inconspicuous seeds. **SEASON:** Evergreen, moist tropical. **WHEN TO**

PLANT: Set transplants when available. Set in ground in Zone 9 or warmer. May freeze to ground but will recover from roots if well-established. Cultivate as indoor specimen in colder climates. **LIGHT:** Partial sun to part shade. **SOIL:** Loam-based, humusy, well-drained, moist. **FERTILIZER:** Timed-release with micronutrients at beginning of growing season. **TRAINING:** Use for covering any rough-textured surface such as stone, brick, wood, or bark.

EUONYMUS

Euonymus fortunei var. *radicans*

HABIT: Rootlike holdfasts. **HEIGHT:** To 15 feet. **FOLIAGE:** Evergreen, oval, dark green. **FLOWERS:** Greenish-white, inconspicuous. **SEASON:** All year. **WHEN TO PLANT:** Set transplants when available. Cold- and heat-tolerant within Zones 5 to 9. **LIGHT:** Sun to part shade. **SOIL:** Loam-based, humusy, well-drained, moist. **FERTILIZER:** Timed-release with micronutrients in spring. **TRAINING:** Outstanding ground cover or for covering brick or stone walls.

FICUS

Ficus pumila. Fig ivy, creeping fig.

HABIT: Aerial-root climbers. **HEIGHT:** Almost no limit to area coverage or height. **FOLIAGE:** Evergreen, small, heart-shaped leaves; can grow 2 to 4 inches long on mature plants. **FLOWERS:** Inconspicuous. **SEASON:** All year. **WHEN TO PLANT:** Set transplants when available, in Zones 8–9 and warmer. Elsewhere, maintain as container plant. **LIGHT:** Full sun to part shade. **SOIL:** Loam-based, humusy, well-drained, moist. **FERTILIZER:** Timed-release with micronutrients at beginning of growing season. **TRAINING:** Suited to covering stone and brick walls and widely used for covering moss-filled topiary forms.

GELSEMIUM

Gelsemium sempervirens. Carolina jessamine, Carolina jasmine.

HABIT: Twining stems. **HEIGHT:** 20 to 30 feet. **FOLIAGE:** Evergreen, glossy, light green, leaves 1 to 4 inches long. **FLOWERS:** Tubular, 1 to 2 inches long, single or double, yellow. **FRAGRANCE:** Sweet. **FRUIT:** Resembles the leaves. **SEASON:** Late winter or early spring. **WHEN TO PLANT:** Set transplants when available, in Zones 8–9. Elsewhere, maintain as container plant. **LIGHT:** Full sun to part shade. **SOIL:** Loam-based, humusy, well-drained, moist. **FERTILIZER:** Timed-release with micronutrients in spring. **TRAINING:** Suited to trellis, lattice, and wire fences, and can be used as ground cover. **CAUTION:** All parts of gelsemium are poisonous.

EUONYMUS

GELSEMIUM

GLORIOSA

GLORIOSA

Gloriosa rothschildiana. Climbing lily.

HABIT: Tendril-like leaf tips. **HEIGHT:** 6 to 12 feet. **FOLIAGE:** Lance-shaped, 5 to 7 inches long, tip extending into tendrillike growth. **FLOWERS:** To 3 inches across, the segments reflexed and recurved; red, yellow, and cream, fading to soft rose. **SEASON:** Spring to summer. **WHEN TO PLANT:** Set tubers horizontally, 2 to 3 inches deep at beginning of warm growing season, usually spring. Hardy in ground in Zones 9 and warmer. Elsewhere, dig and store tubers through winter in a moderately-warm, frost-free place. **LIGHT:** Full to part sun. **SOIL:** Loam-based, humusy, well-drained, moist. **FERTILIZER:** Timed-release with micronutrients at beginning of growing season. **TRAINING:** Suited to training on string or wire against a wall or trellis.

HARDENBERGIA

Hardenbergia violacea. Miniature wisteria, lilac vine.

HABIT: Stem-twining. **HEIGHT:** To 10 feet. **FOLIAGE:** Narrowly oval, 1 to 5 inches long. **FLOWERS:** In pendulous racemes, lilac, pink, purple, or white. **FRUIT:** Brownish pods, 1 to 2 inches long, in

fall. **SEASON:** Flowers in spring. **WHEN TO PLANT:** Set transplants, when available, in the ground in Zone 10. Elsewhere, maintain as a container specimen. **LIGHT:** Full to part sun. **SOIL:** Loam-based, humusy, well-drained, moist. **FERTILIZER:** Timed-release with micronutrients at beginning of growing season. **TRAINING:** Suited to airy garden screening, specimen, or ground cover. Prune after flowering.

HEDERA

Hedera canariensis. Canary Island ivy.

H. helix. English ivy.

HABIT: Aerial rootlets. **HEIGHT:** 15 to 30 feet. **FOLIAGE:** Evergreen; leaves triangular and often lobed; yellowish to almost black; some appear silvery. **FLOWERS:** Inconspicuous. **FRUIT:** Globular, black or yellow. **SEASON:** All-year foliage. **WHEN TO PLANT:** Set transplants when available. Different cultivars widely adapted to cold and heat. Canary Island ivy hardy only to Zones 9 to 10. *H. helix* 'Baltica' tolerates extreme cold. **LIGHT:** Full sun to full shade. Ivies with variegated foliage need more sun. **SOIL:** Loam-based, humusy, well-drained, moist. **FERTILIZER:** Timed-release with micronutrients at beginning of growing season. **TRAINING:** Covers ground, walls of brick and stone. Limited coverage of a tree trunk can be charming, but, if unrestrained, an ivy can suffocate a tree.

HIBBERTIA

Hibbertia scandens. Guinea gold vine.

HABIT: Stem-twining. **HEIGHT:** 8 to 10 feet. **FOLIAGE:** Evergreen; waxy leaves to 3 inches long. **FLOWERS:** Resemble single roses, saucer-shaped; bright yellow; to 2 inches. **FRAGRANCE:** Malodorous. **SEASON:** Flowers primarily summer **WHEN TO PLANT:** Suited to ground culture in Zone 10. Containerize elsewhere. **LIGHT:** Full sun to part shade. **SOIL:** Loam-based, humusy, well-drained,

HEDERA

evenly moist in summer, less so in fall to spring. **FERTILIZER:** Timed-release with micronutrients at beginning of growing season. **TRAINING:** Ideal for covering stone or tile walls or as ground cover. Also recommended for trellis training or against a low fence for a small garden.

HOYA

Hoya carnosa. Wax flower.

HABIT: Aerial rootlets. **HEIGHT:** 10 to 15 feet. **FOLIAGE:** Evergreen; oval shaped, 2 to 4 inches long. **FLOWERS:** Small, in big clusters; white, with pink star centers. **FRAGRANCE:** Honey/vanilla. **FRUIT:** After flowers fall, a spurlike growth remains that should not be dead-headed because it will produce more blooms in succeeding seasons. **SEASON:** Summer-flowering. **WHEN TO PLANT:** Suited to ground culture in Zone 10. Elsewhere, maintain as a container specimen. **LIGHT:** Sun to part shade. **SOIL:** Loam-based, humusy, well-drained, moist in summer, on the dry side in winter. **FERTILIZER:** Timed-release with micronutrients at beginning of growing season. **TRAINING:** Ideal outdoors for training on a pillar or trellis, indoors on a wire or vine wreath.

HUMULUS

Humulus lupulus. Common hop.

HABIT: Stem-twining. **HEIGHT:** 15 to 25 feet. **FOLIAGE:** Three- to five-lobed, 3 to 4 inches across, herbaceous. **FLOWERS:** Male and female on separate plants in cones and bracts, 1 to 2 inches long; greenish. **FRAGRANCE:** Fresh pine. **SEASON:** Summer. **WHEN TO PLANT:** Set transplants when available. Cold- and heat-tolerant within Zones 5–9. **LIGHT:** Full to part sun. **SOIL:** Loam-based, humusy, well-drained, lots of water in summer. **FERTILIZER:** Timed-release with micronutrients at beginning of growing season. **TRAINING:** Good for quick screening on trellises, fences, or arbors.

HOYA

HUMULUS

HYDRANGEA

Hydrangea petiolaris. Climbing hydrangea.

HABIT: Aerial rootlets. **HEIGHT:** To 50 feet. **FOLIAGE:** Deciduous; heart-shaped leaves 2 to 4 inches long. **FLOWERS:** In flat clusters, 6 to 10 inches wide; white. **SEASON:** Summer flowers. **WHEN TO PLANT:** Set transplants when available. Cold- and heat-tolerant within Zones 5 to 8. **LIGHT:** Full sun to part shade. **SOIL:** Loam-based, humusy, well-drained, moist. **FERTILIZER:** Timed-release with micronutrients at beginning of growing season. **TRAINING:** Recommended for rough surfaces such as stone or other masonry walls or a tree trunk. Generally suited to exposures facing north, west, or east.

IPOMOEA

Ipomoea alba. Moonflower.

I. nil. Morning glory.

I. quamoclit. Cypress vine.

I. tricolor. Morning glory.

HABIT: Stem-twining. **HEIGHT:** 10 to 30 feet. **FOLIAGE:** Heart-shaped leaves, to 3 inches. **FLOWERS:** Funnel-form, 3 to 6 inches; white, blue, pink, rose, red, violet. **FRAGRANCE:** *I. alba* at night. **SEASON:** Summer to fall. **WHEN TO PLANT:** Set transplants when available, or sow seeds where they will grow in the spring. **LIGHT:** Full sun to half sun. **SOIL:** Loam-based, humusy, well-drained, moist. **FERTILIZER:** Timed-release with micronutrients at beginning of growing season. **TRAINING:** Quick cover for fences, walls, and structures such as arbors and arches. Flowers last longest in cool temperatures and the vines themselves thrive best after summer heat abates.

HYDRANGEA

IPOMOEA

JASMINUM

Jasminum officinale. Common jasmine (Zones 7–9).

J. polyanthum. Pink-and-white jasmine (Zones 9–10).

J. rex. King's jasmine (Zones 8–10).

J. sambac. Arabian jasmine (Zones 9–10).

J. tortuosum. African jasmine (Zones 9–10).

HABIT: Clambering or stem-twining. **HEIGHT:** 15 to 30 feet. **FOLIAGE:** Evergreen; leaves simple and opposite, or composed of three or more leaflets, to 6 inches long. **FLOWERS:** Tubular, lobed, to 2 inches; white (*J. polyanthum* buds and lobe reverses are pink). **FRAGRANCE:** Jasmine. **SEASON:** *J. sambac* and *J. tortuosum* essentially everblooming; the others bloom variously late winter, spring, or summer. **WHEN TO PLANT:** Set transplants when available, in the ground according to hardiness zones listed above with each species. Any jasmine can also be man-aged successfully as a container plant, especially if it can be kept outdoors during frost-free weather. **LIGHT:** Full sun to half sun. **SOIL:** Loam-based, humusy, well-drained, moist. **FERTILIZER:** Timed-release with micronu-trients at the beginning of the growing season. **TRAINING:** Suited to trellis, lattice structures of all kinds, tepee, fence, or wall.

KADSURA

Kadsura japonica. Scarlet kadsura.

HABIT: Stem-twining. **HEIGHT:** 15 to 20 feet. **FOLIAGE:** Evergreen; leaves oval, dark green, to 4 inches long. **FLOWERS:** Inconspicuous, in clusters; creamy white. **FRUIT:** Bright red berries in the fall. **SEASON:** All-year foliage; berries in the fall. **WHEN TO PLANT:** Set transplants when available, in the ground in Zones 7–9. **LIGHT:** Full sun to part shade. **SOIL:** Loam-based, well-drained, moist. **FERTILIZER:** Timed-release with micronu-trients at the beginning of the growing season. **TRAINING:** Ideal for around a pillar or post, against a wall or on a fence, or for a pergola or arbor.

KENNEDIA

Kennedia rubicunda. Dusky coral pea.

HABIT: Twining. **HEIGHT:** To 10 feet. **FOLIAGE:** Evergreen; leaves composed of three oval leaflets. **FLOWERS:** Pea-like in small trusses; coral red. **SEASON:** Flowers spring to summer. **WHEN TO PLANT:** Set transplants when available, in the ground in Zones 9–10 or warmer; elsewhere containerize and keep outdoors in warm weather. **LIGHT:** Full to part sun. **SOIL:** Loam-based, well-drained, moist spring to summer, on the dry side fall to winter. **FERTILIZER:** Timed-release with micronutrients at the beginning of the growing season. **TRAINING:** Needs support such as string trellis or bamboo canes, then showy for a wall or fence; also for a tepee with brush twigs to establish early growth.

LABLAB

Hyacinth bean (formerly *Dolichos lablab*).

HABIT: Twining perennial herb **HEIGHT:** 10 to 20 feet. **FOLIAGE:** Semi-evergreen in frost-free climate, treated as annual in colder areas; trifoliate compound leaves with leaflets to 7 inches, ovate to rhombic. **FLOWERS:** Fragrant, in clusters of 5, purple in *L. purpureus*, white in the variety 'Alba,' along a spike 6 to 8 inches long, reflexed, notched, wings obovate, 10 stamens. **FRUIT:** Matures rapidly as oblique-oblong maroon bean pods to 5x1 inches containing 2 to 7 seeds, edible and tasty when young. **SEASON:** Spring to fall foliage becoming sparse and leggy in late fall or winter. Fruiting intermittently through growth season. **WHEN TO PLANT:** Set transplants when available. Start indoors in colder climates in late winter or in ground, Zone 9 or warmer. Will tolerate light freeze. **LIGHT:** Full sun to part shade. **SOIL:** Loam-based, humusy, well-drained, moist. **FERTILIZER:** Timed-release with micronutrients at beginning of growing season. **TRAINING:** Use for quick cover of lattice, wire-mesh fence, or dead brush from previous year's growth. For culinary purposes, keep on low fence or arbor.

LAPAGERIA

Lapageria rosea. Chilean bellflower.

HABIT: Stem-twining. **HEIGHT:** 10 to 20 feet. **FOLIAGE:** Evergreen; leaves ovate to oblong, leathery, to 4 inches long. **FLOWERS:** Hanging, bell-shaped with overlapping petals, 3 to 4 inches long; rose-red in the species, various pinks to bright red in cultivars; var. *albiflora* is white. **SEASON:** Late spring-fall. **WHEN TO PLANT:** Set transplants when available, in the ground in Zone 9 and warmer; elsewhere manage as a container plant that can be wheeled outdoors for the warm season's duration. **LIGHT:** Part sun to part shade. **SOIL:**

LAPAGERIA

Loam-based, humusy, well-drained, moist. Extra sphagnum peat moss is often suggested, especially in areas given to alkaline water or soil pH above 6.5. **FERTILIZER:** Timed-release with micronutrients at the beginning of the growing season. **TRAINING:** For trellis or fence, pergola, arbor, or wall. In northern climates sometimes trained near the roof of a greenhouse.

LARDIZABALA

Lardizabala biternata.

HABIT: Stem-twining. **HEIGHT:** 10 to 12 feet. **FOLIAGE:** Evergreen; in leaflets of three, six, or nine, to 4 inches long.

FLOWERS: Purple-brown and whitish. **FRUIT:** Oblong, 2 to 3 inches long, purple; winter to spring. **SEASON:** Flowers and fruits winter to spring. **WHEN TO PLANT:** Set transplants when available, in the ground in Zone 10 or warmer. Elsewhere, maintain in a container and place outdoors in warm weather. **LIGHT:** Sun to part shade. **SOIL:** Loam-based, well-drained, moist. **FERTILIZER:** Timed-release with micronutrients at the beginning of the growing season. **TRAINING:** For arbors, pergolas, lattice structures.

TO PLANT: Set transplants when available, being careful not to disturb the roots. In the deep South, seeds of the annuals are started late summer to fall; elsewhere they are planted early, at the time the first lettuce and radish seeds are sown. **LIGHT:** Full sun. **SOIL:** Loam-based, humusy, well-drained, moist. **FERTILIZER:** Timed-release with micronutrients at the beginning of the growing season. **TRAINING:** String trellis or twiggy brush wood is required to guide these tendril-climbers; otherwise, they will sprawl on the ground.

LONICERA

Honeysuckle

HABIT: Stem-twining. **HEIGHT:** 3 to 80 feet. **FOLIAGE:** Deciduous, semievergreen, or evergreen, depending on the species and the severity of the climate. **FLOWERS:** tubular to bell-like, four-lobed lip; white, yellow, pink, purple, coral, rose, or red. **FRAGRANCE:** Honey, not in all species, but pronounced in *L. fragrantissima, L. hildebrandiana, L. japonica, L. nitida, L. periclymenum,* and *L. pileata.* **FRUIT:** A berry, almost any color, depending on the species. **SEASON:** Variously spring to fall or everblooming. **WHEN TO PLANT:** Set transplants when available; locally adapted species for nearly every climate, hot or cold, wet or dry. **LIGHT:** Sunny to half-sunny. **SOIL:** Well-drained, moist; tolerates drought when established. **FERTILIZER:** Timed-release with micronutrients at the beginning of a growing season. **TRAINING:** Young vines may need some initial tying into the trellis or other support; thereafter they are reasonably self-reliant. Overgrown honeysuckle can be summarily chopped or sheared back at the beginning of the growing season.

LONICERA

LYGODIUM

LYGODIUM

Lygodium japonicum. Climbing fern.

HABIT: Stem-twining. **HEIGHT:** 6 to 15 feet. **FOLIAGE:** Evergreen; leaves in much-divided fronds; leaflets have toothed margins. **SEASON:** All year in frost-free climate. **WHEN TO PLANT:** Set transplants when available, in the ground in Zone 9 or warmer. Elsewhere, maintain in a container. **LIGHT:** Part sun to shade. **SOIL:** Loam-based, humusy, well-drained, moist. **FERTILIZER:** Timed-release with micronutrients at the beginning of the growing season. **TRAINING:** Suited to a string trellis or a chain-link fence.

LATHYRUS

Lathyrus grandiflorus. Everlasting pea.

L. latifolius. Perennial pea.

L. odoratus. Sweet pea.

L. tingitanus. Tangier pea.

HABIT: Tendril-climbing. **HEIGHT:** 6 to 12 feet. **FOLIAGE:** Bluish-green, in leaflets, 2 to 4 inches long. **FLOWERS:** Typical pea shape, to 1 inch, in long racemes. **FRAGRANCE:** Usually sweet, but not always. **SEASON:** Sweet pea and Tangier pea bloom primarily in cooler weather, often winter to spring in the subtropics; the others in spring to summer. **WHEN**

MACFADYENA

Macfadyena unguis-cati (Doxantha sp.). Cat's-claw.

HABIT: Climbs by means of hooked, clawlike, forked tendrils. **HEIGHT:** 25 to 40 feet. **FOLIAGE:** Glossy ovals to 2 inches long, in leaflet pairs; usually deciduous. **FLOWERS:** Trumpets, to 2 inches long. **SEASON:** Flowers early spring. **WHEN TO PLANT:** Set transplants when available, in the ground in Zone 9 and warmer; elsewhere, manage as a container plant that can be put outdoors in frost-free weather. **LIGHT:** Full sun. **SOIL:** Loam-based, well-drained, moist to on the dry side. **FERTILIZER:** Timed-release with micronutrients at the beginning of the season. **TRAINING:** Will cling to almost any support—wood, stone, brick, tree trunk. It is worthwhile to cut this vine back hard after flowering. It grows rapidly after this treatment and will bloom all over, from the ground up, rather than mostly at the top of the vine where the flowers may be all but impossible to see.

MANDEVILLA

Mandevilla x amoena (includes 'Alice du Pont').

M. boliviensis. White dipladenia.

M. laxa. Chilean jasmine.

M. sanderi. (includes 'Red Riding Hood').

M. splendens.

HABIT: Stem-twining. **HEIGHT:** 5 to 30 feet. **FOLIAGE:** Evergreen. Oblong, 2 to 4 inches long by half as wide; deeply veined for quilted effect in the cultivar 'Alice du Pont.' **FLOWERS:** Funnelform, showy; white, pink, cherry-red, yellow. **FRAGRANCE:** Honey, in white Chilean jasmine (*M. laxa*). **SEASON:** Blooms in warm weather, even in winter in a greenhouse. **WHEN TO PLANT:** Set transplants when available. Containerize for indoor/outdoor treatment, but suitable

MANDEVILLA

for ground planting in Zone 10. (*M. laxa* reported ground hardy to about 5°F; if frozen or cut to the ground in spring—done on occasion to rejuvenate tangled old growth—it blooms on the new shoots that same season.) **LIGHT:** Sunny to half-sunny. **SOIL:** Humusy, well-drained, moist. **FERTILIZER:** Timed-release with micronutrients at the beginning of the growing season. **TRAINING:** Climbs enthusiastically on a fence, trellis, or tepee.

MANETTIA

Manettia coccinea.

M. cordifolia. Firecracker vine.

M. luteorubra. Brazilian firecracker vine.

HABIT: Stem-twining. **HEIGHT:** 6 to 12 feet. **FOLIAGE:** Herbaceous, oval to

heart- to lance-shaped, 3 to 6 inches long. **FLOWERS:** Narrow tubes, 1 to 2 inches long; usually bright red with a yellow tip, suggesting a lit firecracker. **SEASON:** Variously winter to summer; everblooming in reasonably warm, frost-free, sunny situations. **WHEN TO PLANT:** Set transplants when available, in Zones 9–10 or warmer. Elsewhere, manage as container plants that can be put outdoors in warm weather. **LIGHT:** Full sun to part sun. **SOIL:** Loam-based, humusy, well-drained, moist. **FERTILIZER:** Timed-release with micronutrients at the beginning of the growing season. **TRAINING:** Suited to various structures including wire, lattice, or cane; large potted specimens are sometimes wound around a large wire or vine wreath.

MANSOA

Mansoa alliacea (Pseudocalymma alliaceum). Garlic vine.

HABIT: Tendril-climbing. **HEIGHT:** 10 to 15 feet. **FOLIAGE:** Three-part leaflets; terminal leaflet often a simple tendril. **FLOWERS:** In groups of 6 to 25, dark to pale purple. **FRAGRANCE:** Plant has strong smell of onions. **SEASON:** Winter to spring flowers. **WHEN TO PLANT:** Set transplants in the ground when available, in Zone 10. Elsewhere, maintain as a container specimen. **LIGHT:** Full to

MANETTIA

part sun. **SOIL:** Loam-based, humusy, well-drained, moist. **FERTILIZER:** Timed-release with micronutrients at beginning of growing season. **TRAINING:** Recommended for covering a small trellis or fence.

MASCAGNIA

Mascagnia macroptera. Golden vine.

HABIT: Slender-stemmed shrub amenable to vine treatment. **HEIGHT:** 6 to 12 feet. **FOLIAGE:** Leathery leaves, oblong or lanceolate to ovate, to 2 inches long. **FLOWERS:** Resembling butterfly orchids, each to 1 inch, in showy racemes; yellow. **SEASON:** Summer to fall flowers. **WHEN TO PLANT:** Set transplants when available, in Zones 8–9 or warmer; elsewhere, manage as container plants that can be placed outdoors in warm weather. **LIGHT:** Full sun. **SOIL:** Loam-based, humusy, well-drained, from moist to on the dry side. **FERTILIZER:** Timed-release with micronutrients at the beginning of the growing season. **TRAINING:** Ideal as fence or wall cover, even for covering a steep bank.

MENISPERMUM

Menispermum canadense. Canada moonseed.

HABIT: Stem-twining. **HEIGHT:** To 15 feet. **FOLIAGE:** Deciduous; leaves oval to heart-shaped, three- to seven-lobed. **FLOWERS:** Cup-shaped, small; greenish-yellow. **FRUIT:** Blackish, in clusters. **CAUTION:** poisonous. **SEASON:** Primarily for summer foliage. **WHEN TO PLANT:** Set transplants when available, in the ground in Zones 7–9; in colder regions, manage as a container specimen that can be placed outdoors in warm weather. **LIGHT:** Full to part shade. **SOIL:** Loam-based, humusy, well-drained, moist. **FERTILIZER:** Timed-release with micronutrients at the beginning of the growing season. **TRAINING:** Ground cover or screen in shade where the soil is generally moist or wet; otherwise, too invasive to encourage in a cultivated garden.

MERREMIA

Merremia tuberosa. Hawaiian wood rose.

HABIT: Twining. **HEIGHT:** 20 to 40 feet. **FOLIAGE:** Digitate into seven lobes. **FLOWERS:** Funnel-shaped, to 2 inches; yellow. **FRUIT:** Ivory-brown, primarily ripening in the fall, the popular "Hawaiian wood rose." **SEASON:** Flowers in summer. **WHEN TO PLANT:** Set transplants when available, in the ground in Zone 10 or warmer only. Elsewhere, manage as container specimen that can be moved outdoors when the weather is above 50°F. **LIGHT:** Full sun. **SOIL:**

MENISPERMUM

Loam-based, humusy, well-drained, moist. **FERTILIZER:** Timed-release with micronutrients at the beginning of the growing season. **TRAINING:** Suited to trellis, fence, wall, arbor, pergola, or other garden structure.

MILLETTIA

Millettia reticulata. Evergreen wisteria.

HABIT: Stem-twining. **HEIGHT:** 15 to 30 feet. **FOLIAGE:** Persistent or semiever-green; leaves odd-pinnate, to 3 inches long. **FLOWERS:** Pealike, in dense racemes, to 8 inches; pinkish-blue to dark red-violet and purple. **FRAGRANCE:** Sweet. **FRUIT:** Shapely pods, to 6 inches long. **SEASON:** Flowers summer to fall. **WHEN TO PLANT:** Set transplants when available, in the ground in Zone 8 or warmer; elsewhere, maintain as container specimen that can be kept outdoors in warm weather. **LIGHT:** Full to half sun. **SOIL:** Loam-based, humusy, well-drained, moist. **FERTILIZER:** Timed-release with micronutrients at the beginning of the growing season. **TRAINING:** Suited to strong garden structures—lattice pavilions, arbors, pergolas, and ornate fences. Not as assertive as true wisteria; often more manageable, especially in a small garden.

MITRARIA

Mitraria coccinea.

HABIT: Scrambling climber. **HEIGHT:** To 6 feet. **FOLIAGE:** Evergreen; leaves oval, toothed. **FLOWERS:** Tubular, 1 to 2 inches long; orange-red. **SEASON:** Flowers late spring to summer. **WHEN TO PLANT:** Set transplants when available, in the ground in Zone 10 or warmer. Elsewhere, maintain as a container plant. **LIGHT:** Half sun to half shade. **SOIL:** Loam-based, humusy, well-drained, moist. **FERTILIZER:** Timed-release with micronutrients at the beginning of the growing season. **TRAINING:** Suited to a small trellis or modified espalier for a container frame.

MOMORDICA

Momordica balsamina. Balsam apple.

M. charantia. Balsam pear.

HABIT: Tendril-twining. **HEIGHT:** 15 to 20 feet. **FOLIAGE:** Variously palmate or pedate, dentate or undulate, 2 to 5 inches across. **FLOWERS:** Resembling those of the related cucumber, to 2 inches; yellow. **FRUIT:** Oblong or ovoid, pendulous, 6 to 12 inches long; first green, then yellow-orange, finally bursting open to reveal red seeds. **SEASON:** Summer to fall or any 60- to 90-day period of reasonably warm, sunny weather. **WHEN TO PLANT:** Set transplants when available, where they are to grow, Zone 9 or warmer, with as little disturbance to the roots as possible. Or sow seeds where they are to grow when the weather is warm and settled and the soil has had a chance to warm. Treat as annuals. **LIGHT:** Full to part sun. **SOIL:** Loam-based, humusy, well-drained, moist. **FERTILIZER:** Timed-release with micronutrients at the beginning of the growing season. **TRAINING:** Suited to quick warm-weather cover for fences, walls, up into trees, arbor, trellis, lattice pavilion, pergola.

MUEHLENBECKIA

Muehlenbeckia complexa. Maidenhair vine.

HABIT: Stem-twining. **HEIGHT:** 20 to 30 feet. **FOLIAGE:** Semideciduous; leaves oblong to rounded or fiddle-shaped; purple or silver beneath. **FLOWERS:** Star-shaped, tiny, greenish-white. **FRUIT:** Small, round, waxy, white. **SEASON:** Summer flowers, fall fruit. **WHEN TO PLANT:** Set transplants when available, in Zone 8 or warmer. **LIGHT:** Full sun to half shade. **SOIL:** Loam-based, humusy, well-drained, moist. **FERTILIZER:** Timed-release with micronutrients at beginning of growing season. **TRAINING:** Recommended for beach gardens or as a screen for unsightly objects such as stumps or old rock piles.

MUTISIA

Mutisia decurrens.

HABIT: Tendril-climber. **HEIGHT:** To 10 feet. **FOLIAGE:** Evergreen; narrowly oblong, 3 to 5 inches long. **FLOWERS:** Single, daisy-like heads, 4 to 5 inches across; red or orange. **SEASON:** Summer blooms. **WHEN TO PLANT:** Set transplants when available, in Zones 8–10. Elsewhere, maintain as container specimen. **LIGHT:** Full sun. **SOIL:** Loam-based, well drained, moist. **FERTILIZER:** Timed-release with micronutrients at beginning of growing season. **TRAINING:** Suited to a small trellis, or as an espalier on a garden wall.

PANDOREA

Pandorea jasminoides. Bower plant.

P. pandorana. Wonga-wonga vine.

HABIT: Stem-twining. **HEIGHT:** 20 to 30 feet. **FOLIAGE:** Evergreen; compound leaves, 2 to 3 inches long with 5 to 9 leaflets. **FLOWERS:** Tubular, each to 2 inches long, in small clusters; white, tinged with pink in *P. jasminoides*, yellow-white, spotted with purple in *P. pandorana.* **SEASON:** Flowers in summer to fall. **WHEN TO PLANT:** Set transplants when available, in Zones 9 to 10. Elsewhere, maintain as container specimen. **LIGHT:** Full sun to half shade. **SOIL:** Loam-based, humusy, well-drained, moist. **FERTILIZER:** Timed-release with micronutrients at beginning of growing season. **TRAINING:** Suited to screens, arbors, or ground cover.

PARTHENOCISSUS

Parthenocissus henryana. Silver-veined creeper.

P. quinquefolia. Woodbine, Virginia creeper.

P. tricuspidata. Japanese ivy, Boston ivy.

HABIT: Twisting tendrils, sometimes with sticky disks on tips. **HEIGHT:** 20 to 30 feet. **FOLIAGE:** Deciduous; *P. henryana* and *P. quinquefolia* have five leaflets to 6 inches long, red when unfolding, marked white on the veins, and purplish beneath; *P. tricuspidata* leaves are ovate or rounded, to 8 inches across. **FLOWERS:** Inconspicuous greenish-white **FRUIT:** Dark blue berries. **SEASON:** Spring to fall foliage, turning scarlet or purple in fall. **WHEN TO PLANT:** Set transplants when available. Set *P. henryana* in the ground in Zone 7 or warmer. Set other two in the ground in Zones 3 or 4 to 10. **LIGHT:** Part sun to part shade. **SOIL:** Loam-based, humusy, well-drained, moist. **FERTILIZER:** Timed-release with micronutrients at beginning of growing season. **TRAINING:** Popular for covering buildings, or any solid, rough surface.

PASSIFLORA

Passionflower

HABIT: Tendril-twining. **HEIGHT:** 10 to 30 feet. **FOLIAGE:** Evergreen or deciduous, depending on the species and the climate. Variously palmate, lobed or peltate, 2 to 6 inches across. **FLOWERS:** Extraordinarily complex, involving petals and sepals, filaments, and corona; arranged symmetrically and often in astoundingly precise color patterns; many colors: often blue to lavender or pink, also red, yellow, orange, or white. **FRAGRANCE:** Lacking in some species, but notable in *Passiflora actinia, P. alata, P.* x *alato-caerulea, P. caerulea, P. cincinnatii, P. edulis, P. helleri, P. incarnata, P.* 'Incense,' and *P. quadrangularis.* **FRUIT:** Edible in *P. edulis, P. quadrangularis, P. mollissima, P. lingularis,* and *P. lauriflora.* **SEASON:** Mostly spring and summer, some year round in warmth and abundant sun. **WHEN TO PLANT:** Set transplants when available; some can tolerate cold to Zones 5–6 if protected (*P. caerulea, P.* x *alatocaerulea, P. incarnata,* and *P.* 'Incense'); most are better suited to

PASSIFLORA

warmer climates or to management as indoor/outdoor container plants. **LIGHT:** Sunny to half-sunny. **SOIL:** Well-drained, moist. **FERTILIZER:** Timed-release with micronutrients at the onset of the growing season. **TRAINING:** These vines grow by leaps and bounds, wherever the new growth senses there is something for the tendrils to coil about: trellis, arbor, fence, and tepee; up, over, and through large shrubs, trees, utility poles, and wires.

PERESKIA

Pereskia aculeata. Lemon vine.

HABIT: Climbing/clambering by cactus spines. **HEIGHT:** To 30 feet. **FOLIAGE:** Deciduous; leaves lance-shaped to elliptic or oval, to 3 inches long. **FLOWERS:** 1 to 2 inches across, white, yellow, or pink. **FRAGRANCE:** Yes. **FRUIT:** Yellow, spiny, to 1 inch in diameter. **SEASON:** Summer flowering. **WHEN TO PLANT:** Set transplants when available, in the ground in Zone 9 or warmer. Elsewhere, maintain as container spec-

imen. **LIGHT:** Full sun. **SOIL:** Loam-based, well-drained, moist to on the dry side. **FERTILIZER:** Timed-release with micronutrients at beginning of growing season. **TRAINING:** Suited for screening and as a specimen. Spines, long and sharp, must be treated with caution. Makes an excellent barrier against intruders.

PERIPLOCA

Periploca graeca. Silk vine.

HABIT: Vigorous, stem-twining, woody vines. **HEIGHT:** To 40 feet. **FOLIAGE:** Deciduous; opposite, oval leaves, 5 inches long. **FLOWERS:** Wheel-shaped in clusters, greenish with brownish-purple inside, 1 inch across. **FRAGRANCE:** Not particularly pleasant. **SEASON:** Spring to fall for foliage, flowers in summer. **WHEN TO PLANT:** Set transplants when available, in Zones 6 and warmer. **LIGHT:** Full sun. **SOIL:** Loam-based, humusy, well-drained, moist. **FERTILIZER:** Timed-release with micronutrients at beginning of growing season. **TRAINING:** Fast, temporary shade or screen. Early each spring, carefully train, thin, and prune to maintain a decorative specimen.

PETREA

Petrea volubilis. Purple wreath.

HABIT: Stem-twining. **HEIGHT:** 15 to 30 feet. **FOLIAGE:** Evergreen; elliptic leaves, to 6 inches long. **FLOWERS:** Axillary racemes 3 to 12 inches long, pale blue-lilac to purple or white. **SEASON:** Spring flowers. **WHEN TO PLANT:** Set transplants when available, in the ground to Zone 10 only. Elsewhere, maintain as a container specimen and place outdoors in warm weather. **LIGHT:** Full to part sun. **SOIL:** Loam-based, humusy, well-drained, moist. **FERTILIZER:** Timed-release with micronutrients at beginning of growing season. **TRAINING:** Outstanding for greenhouse or conservatory, or trained on a small trellis for potted specimens.

PHASEOLUS

Phaseolus coccineus. Scarlet runner bean.

HABIT: Stem-twining. **HEIGHT:** 10 to 15 feet. **FOLIAGE:** Bright green, divided into three roundish leaflets, 3 to 5 inches long. **FLOWERS:** In slender clusters, bright scarlet. **FRUIT:** Flattened, dark green pod, edible when young; mature beans can be shelled for cooking, as green limas. **SEASON:** Summer. **WHEN TO PLANT:** Set transplants when available, taking care not to break the roots, or sow the seeds where they are to grow after the weather has warmed and settled. **LIGHT:** Full sun. **SOIL:** Loam-based, humusy, well-drained, moist. **FERTILIZER:** Timed-release with micronutrients at beginning of growing season. **TRAINING:** Quick cover for fences, arbors, porches, and out buildings.

PHILODENDRON

Philodendron scandens. Heart-leaved philodendron.

HABIT: Aerial root climber. **HEIGHT:** 15 to 30 feet. **FOLIAGE:** Evergreen; leaves heart-shaped, to 12 inches long. **FLOWERS:** Tiny, clustered on fingerlike spadix. **SEASON:** All-year tropical foliage. **WHEN TO PLANT:** Set transplants outdoors when available, in Zones 9–10 or warmer. Elsewhere, maintain as a container specimen. **LIGHT:** Half sun to half shade. **SOIL:** Loam-based, humusy, well-drained, moist. **FERTILIZER:** Timed-release with micronutrients at beginning of growing season. **TRAINING:** Suited to training on any rough surface to which the air roots can attach themselves.

PILEOSTEGIA

Pileostegia viburnoides. Tanglehead.

HABIT: Aerial roots. **HEIGHT:** 30 to 45 feet. **FOLIAGE:** Evergreen; leaves elliptic, 5 to 6 inches long, dark green and glossy. **FLOWERS:** In loose clusters, small, white. **SEASON:** Fall for flowers. **WHEN TO PLANT:** Set transplants when available, in Zone 7 or warmer. Elsewhere, maintain as a container specimen. **LIGHT:** Half sun to full shade. **SOIL:** Loam-based, humusy, well-drained, moist. **FERTILIZER:** Timed-

PHASEOLUS

release with micronutrients at beginning of growing season. **TRAINING:** Recommended for covering stone or brick walls, or as a specimen for garden accent.

PIPER

Piper ornatum. Pepper.

P. porphyrophyllum.

HABIT: Stem-twining shrub, spreading, creeping, or weakly climbing. **HEIGHT:** 15 to 20 feet. **FOLIAGE:** Evergreen; leaves heart-shaped, 3 to 6 inches long, patterned with network of pink or silver veins. **FLOWERS:** Inconspicuous, cylindrical spikes. **SEASON:** All year for foliage. **WHEN TO PLANT:** Set transplants when available, in Zone 10 only. Elsewhere, maintain as a container specimen. **LIGHT:** Half sun to half shade. **SOIL:** Loam-based, humusy, well-drained, moist. **FERTILIZER:** Timed-release with micronutrients at beginning of growing season. **TRAINING:** Recommended for greenhouse or conservatory, or as a container specimen outdoors in warm weather.

PLUMBAGO

Plumbago auriculata (P. capensis). Leadwort.

HABIT: Semiclimber/clamberer. **HEIGHT:** 15 to 20 feet. **FOLIAGE:** Leaves light to medium green, 1 to 2 inches long. **FLOWERS:** Flowers in phloxlike clusters, each to 1 inch wide, light blue or white. **SEASON:** Flowers spring to fall or all year in warm, frost-free climates. **WHEN TO PLANT:** Set transplants when available, in the ground in Zone 9 or warmer. Elsewhere, maintain as a container specimen. **LIGHT:** Full to part sun. **SOIL:** Loam-based, humusy, well-drained, moist. Will tolerate poor soil. **FERTILIZER:** Timed-release with micronutrients at beginning of growing season. **TRAINING:** Recommended for covering a bank, fence, or wall; also suitable as a background or filler plant.

POLYGONUM

Polygonum aubertii. Silver lace-vine.

HABIT: Twining leaf-stems. **HEIGHT:** 20 to 40 feet. **FOLIAGE:** Deciduous; leaves oval to lance-shaped, 2 to 3 inches long. **FLOWERS:** In long, erect, panicled racemes, white. **FRAGRANCE:** Sweet. **SEASON:** Flowers late summer. **WHEN TO PLANT:** Set transplants in the ground when available in Zones 4–9. **LIGHT:** Full sun. **SOIL:** Loam-based, humusy, well-drained, moist. **FERTILIZER:** Timed-release with micronutrients at beginning of growing season. **TRAINING:** High-speed cover for walls, tree trunks, and garden structures. For best appearance, train, prune, and thin out in spring before new growth begins.

PUERARIA

Pueraria lobata. Kudzu vine.

HABIT: Stem-twining, smothering, invasive, aggressive grower. **HEIGHT:** 60 feet or more. **FOLIAGE:** Deciduous, trifoliate leaflets ovoid to rhomboid, to 6 inches long. **FLOWERS:** Long, dense clusters, pealike, purple. **FRAGRANCE:** Sweet. **FRUIT:** Hairy, to 4 inches long. **SEASON:** Summer for flowers. **WHEN TO PLANT:** Notoriously hardy, Zones 5–10. Probably best not to introduce to any garden south of Zone 7. **LIGHT:** Full to part sun. **SOIL:** Well-drained, moist. **FERTILIZER:** Probably not needed. **TRAINING:** Quick massive screening.

PYROSTEGIA

Pyrostegia venusta. Flame vine.

HABIT: Disc-tipped twining tendrils. **HEIGHT:** 25 to 40 feet. **FOLIAGE:** Leaflets oval, to 3 inches long. **FLOWERS:** To 3 inches long, reddish orange. **SEASON:** Winter to spring for flowers. **WHEN TO PLANT:** Set transplants when available, in Zone 10. Elsewhere, maintain as a container specimen. **LIGHT:** Full to half sun. **SOIL:** Loam-based, humusy, well-drained, moist. **FERTILIZER:** Timed-release with micronutrients at begin-

ning of growing season. **TRAINING:** Recommended as an arbor or roof vine in a frost-free climate.

QUISQUALIS

Quisqualis indica. Rangoon creeper.

HABIT: Clamberer; loose, lax stems. **HEIGHT:** 20 to 30 feet. **FOLIAGE:** Leaves opposite, simple, to 5 inches long. **FLOWERS:** Terminal, drooping spikes, slender tubes to 3 inches long, green and white, changing to pink or red. **FRAGRANCE:** Orange blossom. **FRUIT:** Dry, five-winged. **SEASON:** Flowers late spring to fall. **WHEN TO PLANT:** Set transplants when available, in the ground in Zones 9–10 or warmer. Maintain elsewhere in container. **LIGHT:** Full to half sun. **SOIL:** Loam-based, humusy, well-drained, moist. **FERTILIZER:** Timed-release with micronutrients at beginning of growing season. **TRAINING:** Suited to a trellis, arbor, or pergola. Loose, lax stems need tying to supports.

POLYGONUM

QUISQUALIS

RHODOCHITON

RHODOCHITON

Rhodochiton volubile. Purple bell vine.

HABIT: Coiling leaf-stems. **HEIGHT:** 5 to 10 feet. **FOLIAGE:** Soft, fuzzy, to 3 inches. **FLOWERS:** Nodding, tubular, purple-red. **SEASON:** Summer blooming. **WHEN TO PLANT:** Set transplants when available at beginning of growing season, or start seeds early indoors in a warm, sunny place. Ground hardy in Zone 8. Treat as annual in colder regions or winter in a warm place. **LIGHT:** Full to half sun. **SOIL:** Loam-based, humusy, well-drained, moist. **FERTILIZER:** Timed-release with micronutrients at beginning of growing season. **TRAINING:** Suited to covering a low fence or trellis. Also for a 6-foot tepee or similar form.

ROSA

Rose

HABIT: Thorn-climbers/clamberers. **HEIGHT:** 10 to 30 feet. **FOLIAGE:** Deciduous leaflets, except notably evergreen in Lady Banks rose (*Rosa banksiae*) and *R. bracteata* 'Mermaid.' **FLOWERS:** Single or double, miniature to large flowers, borne singly or in clusters, at the tips and from the lateral branches; all colors except blue. **FRAGRANCE:** Not in all species, but the most popular climbing roses tend to be fragrant: for example: 'New Dawn' (blush pink), 'Crimson Glory' Climbing, 'Fragrant Cloud' Climbing

(coral-red), 'Sutter's Gold' Climbing, and 'Paul's Lemon Pillar' (creamy-white). **FRUIT:** Seed hips can turn glowing golden yellow to any hue of orange or red, remaining showy through fall and early winter. **SEASON:** Species and older varieties and Ramblers may bloom once annually, late spring to early summer; most climbing roses are everblooming. **WHEN TO PLANT:** Set containerized transplants when available; plant bareroot stock in early spring. Roses are widely cold- and heat-tolerant; in areas having temperature extremes, select locally recommended climbers. **LIGHT:** Half a day or more of sun. **SOIL:** Well-drained and evenly moist, although *Rosa* is relatively drought-tolerant when established. **FERTILIZER:** All-purpose timed-release with micronutrients or a special product labeled for roses; spring, summer, early fall. **TRAINING:** During first two seasons, remove only the dead wood. Thereafter, annually remove one-fifth to one-third of the oldest or bloomed-out canes, back to the ground or from the point where the cane seems to have originated. Roses that bloom once at the beginning of the season, Ramblers for example, are never pruned until after they finish flowering. Climbing roses can be thinned in late winter or early spring. In either case, the main young canes are tied in to the support or wound around pillars and posts in order to position as much growth as possible parallel to the ground; this horizontalization stimulates the formation of many lateral branches, each a virtual bloom factory. Rank-growing roses in general can be managed as climbers. There are even miniatures that can qualify, such as the old-fashioned sweetheart rose, 'Climbing Cecile Brunner.' It can grow 20 to 30 feet tall and produce profuse clusters of small, light pink, fragrant flowers from late spring to fall frost, even through winter in warm places. "Natural" climbers such as 'Paul's

ROSA

Scarlet' and 'New Dawn' are distinguished from climbing sports of modern large-flowered (Hybrid Tea and Grandiflora) and cluster-flowered (Floribunda) hybrids.

SCHISANDRA

Schisandra chinensis. Magnolia vine.

HABIT: Stem-twining. **HEIGHT:** 15 to 20 feet. **FOLIAGE:** Leaves oblong, elliptic, to 4 inches long. **FLOWERS:** On pedicles 1 to 2 inches long, white or pinkish. **FRAGRANCE:** Vanilla. **FRUIT:** Brilliant red berries in drooping clusters. **SEASON:** Fall berries. **WHEN TO PLANT:** Set transplants when available, in the ground in Zones 5–9. Both male and female plants are required to ensure a berry crop. **LIGHT:** Half sun to half shade. **SOIL:** Loam-based, humusy, well-drained, moist. **FERTILIZER:** Timed-release with micronutrients at beginning of growing season. **TRAINING:** Recommended for screening, shade on a pergola, or as a garden accent.

SCHIZOPHRAGMA

Schizophragma hydrangeoides. Japanese hydrangea vine.

HABIT: Aerial rootlets. **HEIGHT:** 25 to 30 feet. **FOLIAGE:** Deciduous; leaves broadly ovate, to 4 inches long. **FLOWERS:** In flat clusters, resembling true climbing hydrangea; white. **SEASON:** Midsummer flowering. **WHEN TO PLANT:** Set transplants when available, in the ground in

Zones 5–8. **LIGHT:** Half sun to half shade. **SOIL:** Loam-based, humusy, well-drained, moist. **FERTILIZER:** Timed-release with micronutrients at beginning of growing season. **TRAINING:** Looks best against a rough stone wall. Young plants need cane supports to help them establish quickly.

SECHIUM

Sechium edule. Chayote, vegetable pear.

HABIT: Tall climber with running stems. **HEIGHT:** 15 to 20 feet. **FOLIAGE:** Deciduous; lobed leaves, to 10 inches long. **FLOWERS:** Small, funnel-shaped; white. **FRUIT:** Pear-shaped (obovate pyriform) and furrowed; green or white; to 4 inches; edible. **SEASON:** Summer to fall for fruit. **WHEN TO PLANT:** Set transplants when available, at beginning of long, warm growing season. It is also possible to grow the vines from whole, ripe fruits, planted in spring with the wide end in the soil and the stem slightly exposed. **LIGHT:** Full sun. **SOIL:** Loam-based, humusy, well-drained, moist. **FERTILIZER:** Timed-release with micronutrients at beginning of growing season. **TRAINING:** For quick screening on a fence or lattice.

SENECIO

Senecio confusus. Orange-glow vine.

HABIT: Stem-twining. **HEIGHT:** To 20 feet. **FOLIAGE:** Evergreen; to 2 inches long. **FLOWERS:** Profuse, small, orange-red, daisylike, in large clusters. **SEASON:** Variable, blooming all year in frost-free regions. **WHEN TO PLANT:** Set transplants when available, in the ground in Zones 9–10. Elsewhere, maintain as container specimen. **LIGHT:** Full sun to partial shade. **SOIL:** Loam-based, humusy, well-drained, moist. **FERTILIZER:** Timed-release with micronutrients at beginning of growing season. **TRAINING:** Makes a suitably colorful screen with a mass of slender intertwining stems. Excellent for fences, trellises, arbors, or pergolas.

SCHISANDRA

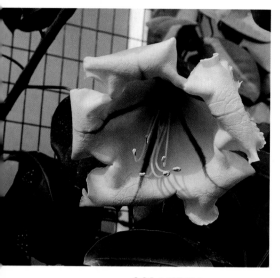

SOLANDRA

Solandra grandiflora (S. nitida). Chalice vine.

HABIT: Clamberers/climbers. **HEIGHT:** 15 to 30 feet. **FOLIAGE:** Evergreen; oval shaped, to 5 inches long. **FLOWERS:** Trumpet-shaped, to 10 inches across; golden yellow with purple-brown stripes. **FRAGRANCE:** Honey. **SEASON:** Blooms winter, spring, and fall in warm climates. **WHEN TO PLANT:** Set transplants when available, in the ground in Zone 10. Elsewhere, maintain as container specimen. **LIGHT:** Full to half sun. **SOIL:** Loam-based, humusy, well-drained, moist. **FERTILIZER:** Timed-

release with micronutrients at beginning of growing season. **TRAINING:** Recommended for large space with a strong trellis onto which the wandering stems can be regularly tied and guided.

SOLANUM

Solanum jasminoides. Potato vine, jasmine nightshade.

S. seaforthianum. St. Vincent lilac, Italian jasmine.

HABIT: Climbers via curled leaf stems. **HEIGHT:** 18 to 20 feet. **FOLIAGE:** Deciduous; entire or divided into lobes, to 3 inches long. **FLOWERS:** In clusters, star-shaped, white to blue. **FRAGRANCE:** Sweet. **FRUIT:** Branching clusters of showy red berries, edible for birds but not people. **SEASON:** More or less everblooming in warm weather. **WHEN TO PLANT:** Set transplants when available, in the ground in Zone 9 or warmer. Elsewhere, maintain as container specimen. **LIGHT:** Full to part sun. **SOIL:** Loam-based, humusy, well-drained, moist. **FERTILIZER:** Timed-release with micronutrients at beginning of growing season. **TRAINING:** Suited to covering walls, fences, arbors, and pergolas. These clamberers need tying to supports to guide growth. Prune in spring to maintain desired shape.

STAUNTONIA

Stauntonia hexaphylla.

HABIT: Stem-twining. **HEIGHT:** To 40 feet. **FOLIAGE:** Evergreen; to 4 inches long, arranged finger-fashion in 3 to 7 leaflets. **FLOWERS:** Whitish male flowers, to about 1 inch long, purplish female flowers, in clusters, on separate plants. **FRAGRANCE:** Violet. **SEASON:** Early summer for flowers. **WHEN TO PLANT:** Set transplants when available, in the ground in Zones 8–10. Elsewhere, maintain as a container specimen. **LIGHT:** Half sun to half shade. **SOIL:**

Loam-based, humusy, well-drained, moist. **FERTILIZER:** Timed-release with micronutrients at beginning of growing season. **TRAINING:** Recommended for screening or shading for fence, wall, arbor, or pergola.

STEPHANOTIS

Stephanotis floribunda. Madagascar jasmine.

HABIT: Twining stems. **HEIGHT:** 10 to 15 feet. **FOLIAGE:** Evergreen; opposite, leathery leaves, glossy, dark-green, to 4 inches long. **FLOWERS:** Funnel-shaped, waxy, 1 to 2 inches long, in open clusters. **FRAGRANCE:** Orange blossom.

FRUIT: Egg-shaped, to 2 inches long. **SEASON:** Spring to summer. **WHEN TO PLANT:** Set transplants when available, in the ground in Zone 10. Elsewhere, maintain as a container specimen. **LIGHT:** Ideal: shaded roots and tops in full sun. **SOIL:** Loam-based, humusy, well-drained, moist. **FERTILIZER:** Timed-release with micronutrients at beginning of growing season. **TRAINING:** Suitable for trellis, arbor, or pergola.

STIGMAPHYLLON

Stigmaphyllon ciliatum. Butterfly vine.

HABIT: Stem-twining. **HEIGHT:** 12 to 15 feet. **FOLIAGE:** Evergreen. **FLOWERS:** Small, yellow, in loose clusters. **FRAGRANCE:** Not fragrant. **FRUIT:** Butterfly-shaped, lime-green. **SEASON:** Spring or summer, sometimes fall. **WHEN TO PLANT:** Set transplants when available, in Zones 8–9, elsewhere grow as an indoor/outdoor container vine on a trellis. **LIGHT:** Sunny to half-sunny. **SOIL:** Well-drained, moist; tolerates drought when established. **FERTILIZER:** Timed-release with micronutrients at the beginning of the growing season. **TRAINING:** Needs little encouragement to take hold on a trellis, fence, arbor, or tepee.

STRONGYLODON

Strongylodon macrobotrys. Jade vine.

HABIT: Stem-twining. **HEIGHT:** 30 to 40 feet. **FOLIAGE:** Evergreen, pink-bronze at first, in leaflets, to 5 inches long. **FLOWERS:** In pendant racemes, to 3 feet; each flower to 3 inches long, bluish-green. **SEASON:** Spring-blooming. **WHEN TO PLANT:** Set transplants when available, in the ground in Zone 10. Elsewhere, maintain as a container specimen. **LIGHT:** Full to part sun. **SOIL:** Loam-based, humusy, well-drained, moist. **FERTILIZER:** Timed-release with micronutrients at beginning of growing season. **TRAINING:** Showy, bold, vigorous, for screening or shade, on suitably strong structures.

STRONGYLODON

SYNGONIUM

Syngonium podophyllum. Arrow-head vine.

HABIT: Aerial root-climbing or creeping. **HEIGHT:** 10 to 15 feet. **FOLIAGE:** Evergreen, arrow-shaped, light green, sometimes variegated with silver, pink, or white. **FLOWERS:** Inconspicuous, rare except in the tropics. **SEASON:** Tropical foliage all year. **WHEN TO PLANT:** Set transplants in the ground when available, in Zone 9 or warmer. Elsewhere, maintain as container specimen. **LIGHT:** Half sun to shade. **SOIL:** Loam-based, humusy, well-drained, moist. **FERTILIZER:** Timed-release with micronutrients at beginning of growing season. **TRAINING:** Useful for clothing stone, brick, or other masonry walls in subtropical or warmer garden.

TECOMARIA

Tecomaria capensis. Cape honeysuckle.

HABIT: Shrub with climbing tendencies. **HEIGHT:** 15 to 25 feet. **FOLIAGE:** Evergreen; leaves divided into many green leaflets. **FLOWERS:** Tubular, 2 inches, in pendant clusters, orange-red; cultivars available in salmon-rose, orange, gold, and yellow. **SEASON:** Primarily summer and fall. **WHEN TO PLANT:** Set transplants when available, in the ground in Zone 9 and warmer. Elsewhere, maintain as container specimen. **LIGHT:** Full sun. **SOIL:** Loam-based, humusy, well-drained, moist. **FERTILIZER:** Timed-release with micronutrients at beginning of growing season. **TRAINING:** If tied to supports, suited to covering a wall, trellis, arbor, or pergola.

TETRASTIGMA

Tetrastigma voinieranum. Chestnut vine.

HABIT: Tendril climber. **HEIGHT:** 40 to 60 feet. **FOLIAGE:** Evergreen; 3 to 5 leaflets, 4 to 8 inches long. **FLOWERS:** Inconspicuous. **SEASON:** All-year tropical

SYNGONIUM

TETRASTIGMA

TRACHELOSPERMUM

foliage. **WHEN TO PLANT:** Set transplants when available, in the ground in Zone 10. Elsewhere, maintain as a container specimen. **LIGHT:** Half sun to half shade. **SOIL:** Loam-based, humusy, well-drained, moist. **FERTILIZER:** Timed-release with micronutrients at beginning of growing season. **TRAINING:** Rapid cover for tropical walls and fences.

THLADIANTHA

Thladiantha dubia (a cucurbit).

HABIT: Tendril climber. **HEIGHT:** 10 to 15 feet. **FOLIAGE:** Deciduous; oval to heart-shaped, to 4 inches long. **FLOWERS:** Bell-shaped, to 2 inches; yellow. **SEASON:** Summer-flowering. **WHEN TO PLANT:** Set transplants in the ground when available, in Zone 7 or warmer. Elsewhere, maintain as a container specimen. **LIGHT:** Full sun. **SOIL:** Loam-based, humusy, well-drained, moist. **FERTILIZER:** Timed-release with micronutrients at beginning of growing season. **TRAINING:** For quick cover of fences, walls, or any lattice garden structure.

THUNBERGIA

Thunbergia grandiflora. Blue trumpet or blue sky vine.

HABIT: Stem-twining. **HEIGHT:** 20 to 30 feet. **FOLIAGE:** Evergreen. Triangular-ovate, to 2 inches long by half as wide. **FLOWERS:** Lobed, tubular; in showy sprays of blue or white. **SEASON:** Fall, winter, spring in mild climates and greenhouses. **WHEN TO PLANT:** Set transplants when available, Zones 8–10; in colder places, it may be grown in a large pot or tub and wintered over in a cool, frost-free place. **LIGHT:** Sunny to half-sunny. **SOIL:** Loam-based, humusy, well-drained, moist; tolerates drought when established. **FERTILIZER:** Timed-release with micronutrients at the beginning of a growing season. **TRAINING:** Needs little guidance in twining around bamboo or chain-link fence.

TRACHELOSPERMUM

Trachelospermum jasminoides. Star jasmine, Confederate jasmine.

HABIT: Semitwining and aerial rootlets. **HEIGHT:** 15 to 20 feet. **FOLIAGE:** Dark, glossy; evergreen. **FLOWERS:** Starry, in small clusters; white or pale yellow. **FRAGRANCE:** Jasmine scented. **SEASON:** Spring; intermittently in summer to fall. **WHEN TO PLANT:** Set transplants when available. Cold- and heat-tolerance for Zones 8 to 9; *T. jasminoides* 'Madison' is suited for Zones 7 to 10. **LIGHT:** Half-sunny to shady. **SOIL:** Humusy, well-drained, moist.

TROPAEOLUM

FERTILIZER: Timed-release with micron trients at the onset of the growing season. **TRAINING:** Prune lightly to shape after the main flowering. Beginning vines may need to be tied in place. The Asiatic *T. asiaticum* (yellow flowers in summer), a.k.a. *Rhynchospermum*, is often used as a ground cover, but if provided a mesh screen it will climb quickly to almost any height.

TROPAEOLUM

Tropaeolum tricolorum. Climbing nasturtium.

HABIT: Leaf-stem twining. **HEIGHT:** 15 to 20 feet. **FOLIAGE:** Five- to seven-lobed, 1 to 2 inches across. **FLOWERS:** Small, pouched, with anterior spur, combining orange-red-yellow and black. **SEASON:** Spring, early summer flowers. **WHEN TO PLANT:** Set transplants or tubers when available, at beginning of growing season; hardy only in Zone 8. Elsewhere, maintain as container specimen. **LIGHT:** Full sun, not heat-tolerant. **SOIL:** Loam-based, humusy, well-drained, moist. **FERTILIZER:** Timed-release with micronutrients at beginning of growing season. **TRAINING:** Does best when encouraged to scramble over hedge or neighboring shrub. Also suited to training on a small trellis.

VITIS

Vitis. Grape vine.

HABIT: Discs or tendril climbers. **HEIGHT:** 20 to 40 feet. **FOLIAGE:** Deciduous; three- or five-lobed, 5 to 12 inches long; dark green, turning red and purple in fall. **FLOWERS:** Inconspicuous in summer. **FRUIT:** If growing the vine for edible grapes, select only cultivars recommended for your region. **SEASON:** Foliage attractive spring to fall except in regions plagued by Japanese beetles. **WHEN TO PLANT:** Set transplants when available at beginning of growing season, using species locally adapted to extremes of heat and cold. **LIGHT:** Full sun. **SOIL:** Loam-based, humusy, well-drained, moist. **FERTILIZER:** Timed-release with micronutrients at beginning of growing season. **TRAINING:** Suited to all types of screening, shading, and embellishing of garden structures—rustic to formal or classical.

WISTERIA

Wisteria floribunda. Japanese wisteria.

W. sinensis. Chinese wisteria.

HABIT: Twining stems. **HEIGHT:** *W. floribunda*, 20 to 30 feet; *W. sinensis*, 30 to 50 feet. **FOLIAGE:** Deciduous; in leaflets, 3 to 8 inches long. **FLOWERS:** In clusters, 12 to 18 inches long. **FRAGRANCE:** Sweet. **FRUIT:** Velvety pods, 6 to 7 inches long. **SEASON:** Flowers in late spring. **WHEN TO PLANT:** Set transplants in ground when available, in Zones 5 to

WISTERIA

10. Wisteria adapts well to container culture and to bonsai treatment. **LIGHT:** Full sun. **SOIL:** Loam-based, humusy, well-drained, moist. **FERTILIZER:** Timed-release with micronutrients at beginning of growing season. **TRAINING:** Recommended for arbors, pergolas, large trees, and facade trellises that outline architectural components. To encourage blooming, prune lateral shoots in late summer back to five leaves or fewer. This treatment may be repeated in winter, toward the formation of strong-flowering spurs.

VITIS

Sources and Bibliography

ANTIQUE ROSE EMPORIUM
Rt. 5, Box 143
Brenham, TX 77833
catalog $4
Old climbing roses.

APPALACHIAN GARDENS
Box 82
Waynesboro, PA 17268
Uncommon woodies.

BEAVER CREEK NURSERY
Box 18243
Knoxville, TN 37928
catalog $1
Uncommon woodies.

BURPEE, W. ATLEE CO.
300 Park Ave.
Warminster, PA 18974
Something for everyone, not necessarily rare—or common.

CAMELLIA FOREST NURSERY
125 Carolina Forest
Chapel Hill, NC 27514
list $1
Uncommon woodies.

CANYON CREEK NURSERY
3527 Dry Creek Rd.
Oroville, CA 95965
Silver-leaved plants; plants for Xeriscaping.

CURTIS, PHILLIP, FARMS
P.O. Box 640
Canby, OR 97013
Woodies and herbaceous plants of note.

DODD'S, TOM, RARE PLANTS
Drawer 95
Semmes, AL 36575
list $1
Trees, shrubs, vines, extremely select.

DOGWOOD HILLS NURSERY
Rt. 3, Box 181
Franklinton, LA 70438
catalog $2
Uncommon plants.

FLORA LAN NURSERY
Rt. 1, Box 357
Forest Grove, OR 97116
Uncommon woodies.

FOREST FARM
990 Tetherow Rd.
Williams, OR 97544-9599
catalog $3
Fascinating woody plants in small sizes.

GEORGE, D.S., NURSERIES
2491 Penfield
Fairport, NY 14450
list 50 cents
Clematis.

GLASSHOUSE WORKS GREENHOUSES
Church St., P.O. Box 97
Stewart, OH 45778-0097
catalog $5
Leading collection of plants for container gardening, indoors and out, including many vines.

GREER GARDENS
1280 Goodpasture Island Rd.
Eugene, OR 97401
catalog $3
Uncommon woodies.

HASTINGS, H.G., CO.
Box 4274
Atlanta, GA 30302
Old, new, rare, common, ornamental, edible.

HERITAGE ROSARIUM
211 Haviland Mill Rd.
Brookville, MD 20833
list $1
Old roses.

HERITAGE ROSE GARDENS
16831 Mitchell Creek Dr.
Fort Bragg, CA 95437
catalog $1
Old roses.

HIGH COUNTRY ROSARIUM
1717 Downing St.
Denver, CO 80218
Old roses.

HOLBROOK FARM AND NURSERY
P.O. Box 368
Fletcher, NC 28732
*Worthy woodies and other select
plants.*

HUDSON, J.L., SEEDSMAN
Box 1058
Redwood City, CA 94064
catalog $1
*Flowers, nonhybrid vegetables,
herbs.*

HUGHES NURSERY
1305 Wynooche W.
Montesano, WA 98563
$1.50 for list
Uncommon woodies.

KARTUZ GREENHOUSES
1408 Sunset Dr.
Vista, CA 92083
catalog $2
*Large collection of begonias, gesner-
iads, miniature houseplants, vines,
especially Passiflora.*

LAMB NURSERIES
E. 101 Sharp Ave.
Spokane, WA 99202
Outstanding for perennials.

LOGEE'S GREENHOUSES
141 North St.
Danielson, CT 06239
catalog $3
*All manner of unusual plants for
pots and gardens, indoors and out,
exotic vines.*

LOUISIANA NURSERY
Rt. 7, Box 43
Opelousas, LA 70570
catalog $2
Uncommon woodies.

LOWE'S OWN ROOT ROSES
6 Sheffield Rd.
Nashua, NH 03062
catalog $2
Old roses.

MELLINGER'S
2310 W. South Range Rd.
North Lima, OH 44452-9731
*All kinds of plants, woody, herba-
ceous, ornamental, edible.*

MERRY GARDENS
Camden, ME 04843
list $1, *Herbs, pelargoniums,
cultivars of Hedera helix.*

MILAEGER'S GARDENS
4838 Douglas Ave.
Racine, WI 53402
catalog $1, *Perennials.*

NICHE GARDENS
1111 Dawson Rd.
Chapel Hill, NC 27516
catalog $3
Perennials.

NORTH CAROLINA STATE UNIVERSITY
ARBORETUM
Box 7609
Raleigh, NC 27695
Membership permits participation in worthy plant propagation and dissemination.

PARK, GEO. W., SEED CO.
Greenwood, SC 29647
Something for everyone—new, old, rare, common.

PLANTS OF THE SOUTHWEST
1812 Second St.
Santa Fe, NM 87501
catalog $2

ROCKY MOUNTAIN RARE PLANTS
Box 20092
Denver, CO 80220
list $1
Perennials.

ROSES OF YESTERDAY AND TODAY
Brown's Valley Rd.
Watsonville, CA 95076
catalog $2
Old roses.

ROSLYN NURSERY
211 Burrs Lane
Dix Hills, NY 11746
catalog $2
Woodies, perennials.

SISKIYOU RARE PLANT NURSERY
2825 Cummings Rd.
Medford, OR 97501
catalog $2

STEFFEN, ARTHUR H.
Box 184
Fairport, NY 14450
Clematis.

THOMPSON & MORGAN
Box 1308
Jackson, NJ 08527
Rare and common seeds for all kinds of plants.

TRANS PACIFIC NURSERY
29870 Mill Creek Rd.
Sheridan, OR 97378
Uncommon woodies.

WAYSIDE GARDENS
One Garden Lane
Hodges, SC 29695-0001
Trees, shrubs, vines, herbaceous perennials, ornamental grasses, bulbs, tubers, corms, rhizomes.

WE-DU NURSERY
Rt. 5, Box 724
Marion, NC 28752
catalog $2
Outstanding woody and herbaceous plants.

WHITE FLOWER FARM
Litchfield, CT 06759
catalog $5
Woodies, vines, perennials, bulbs.

WOODLANDERS
1128 Colleton Ave.
Aiken, SC 29801
catalog $1.50
Worthy woodies, hardy Passiflora.

YUCCA DO NURSERY
P.O. Box 655
Waller, TX 77484
catalog $3
Cutting-edge natively adapted plants, vines included, many collected in ongoing expeditions to Mexico.

AMERICAN WOOD COLUMN
913 Grand St.
Brooklyn, NY 11211
(718) 782-3163
Wood turnings, moldings, and columns.

BAMBOO FENCER
31 Germania St.
Jamaica Plain, MA 02130
(617) 524-6137
FAX (617) 524-3596
Custom bamboo structures: fences, gates, trellises, arbors.

BOSTON TURNING WORKS
42 Plympton St.
Boston, MA 02118
(617) 482-9085
FAX (617) 482-0415
Finials of all kinds.

BOW BENDS
P.O. Box 9009
Bolton, MA 01740
(508) 779-6464
Exotic gazebos, bridges, arbors.

CINCINNATI ARTISTIC WROUGHT IRON
2943 Eastern Ave.
Cincinnati, OH 45226
(513) 321-5429
Custom design ironwork.

CLASSIC ARCHITECTURAL SPECIALTIES
3223 Canton St.
Dallas, TX 75226
(214) 748-1668
Reproduction millwork, including finials of all kinds.

FEATURED CRAFTSMEN

JOE SMILEY
EXTERIOR WOODWORKS
11044 Boston Road
North Royalton, OH 44133
(216) 582-5884

TIM DUVAL
PLANT SPECIALISTS, INC.
42-25 Vernon Blvd.
Long Island City, NY 11101
(718) 392-9404

DANIEL JANISH
DAN'S CUSTOM
WOODWORKING
1322 1/2 Nicholson Rd.
Houston, TX 77008
(713) 861-3659

LOREN CHARTER
VILLAGE WOODWORKS
P.O. Box 801781
Houston, TX 77280-1781
(713) 468-6439

DAVID ROBINSON
NATURAL EDGE
515 Tuxford Court
Trenton, NJ 08638
(609) 737-8996
Pennington, NJ

COUNTRY CASUAL
17317 Germantown Rd., Suite 409
Germantown, MD 20874-2999
(301) 540-0040
*Modular trellis panels, English solid
teak seats and planter boxes,
wrought iron rose arches.*

DALTON PAVILIONS
7260 Oakley St.
Philadelphia, PA 19111
(215) 342-9804
*Ready-to-assemble red cedar gaze-
bos and lattice structures.*

DOVER METALS CO.
4768 Highway M-63
Coloma, MI 49038
(616) 849-1411
FAX (616)849-2903
*Pyramids, urns, and plant stands in
French-style polished steel wire.
Also, copper over steel and nickel
over steel.*

THE GARDEN ARCHITECTURE GROUP
631 N. Third St.
Philadelphia, PA 19123
(215) 627-5552
*Ready-to-assemble cedar trellis
structures: arbors, screens, wall
appliqués, pergolas.*

GARDEN CONCEPTS COLLECTION
P.O. Box 241233
Memphis, TN 38124-1233
(901) 756-1649
FAX (901) 755-4564
*Custom-crafted latticework and
accessories.*

GARDENER'S SUPPLY COMPANY
128 Intervale Rd.
Burlington, VT 05401
(802) 863-1700
*Arbors and benches in Western red
cedar, metal trellises, cast iron
benches, bamboo tepees.*

GAZEBO CENTRAL
Grand Rapids, MI 49508
1-800-339-0288
*Delicate aluminum gazebos with
powder coat finish.*

KENNETH LYNCH & SONS
Traditional Craftsmen
84 Danbury Rd.
Wilton, CT 06897
(203) 762-8363
FAX (203) 762-2999
*A vast collection of garden orna-
ments: statuary, fountains, pools,
urns, sundials, weather vanes.*

M. R. LABBE, CO.
P.O. Box 467
Biddeford, ME 04005
(207) 282-3420
*Ready-to-assemble red cedar arbors
and trellises.*

NEBRASKA PLASTICS, INC.
P.O. Box 45
Cozad, NE 69130-0045
1-800-445-2887
*Ready-to-assemble rose trellises and
lattice arbors in PVC compounds.*

NEW ENGLAND GARDEN ORNAMENTS
38 E. Brookfield Rd.
North Brookfield, MA 01535
(508) 867-4474
*Free-standing lattice screens with
planter boxes.*

THE PAINTED GARDEN, INC.
304 Edge Hill Rd.
Glenside, PA 19038
(215) 884-7378
*Contemporary-design garden struc-
tures in painted metal.*

ROMANCING THE WOODS, INC.
33 Raycliffe Dr.
Woodstock, NY 12498
(914) 246-6976
FAX (914) 246-1021
Red cedar rustic structures.

RUSTICKS FURNITURE &
ACCESSORIES
13 Chestnut Sq.
P.O. Box 521
Cashiers, NC 28717
(704) 743-3172
FAX (704) 743-2969
*Handcrafted furniture and acces-
sories made to order.*

SOUTHERN SWINGS, INC.
4400 Commerce Circle SW
Atlanta, GA 30336
(404) 505-5910
*Lattice arbors and arbor-supported
swings.*

SUN SOURCE, INC.
P.O. Box 4191
Metuchen, NJ 08840
*Handcrafted redwood arbors,
trellises.*

VINTAGE WOODWORKS
513 S. Adams
Fredericksburg, TX 78624
(512) 997-9513
*A variety of wood products: finials,
balusters, newel posts, ready-to-
assemble gazebos.*

VIXEN HILL GAZEBOS
Elverson, PA 19520
1-800-423-2766
Ready-to-assemble cedar gazebos.

WALPOLE WOODWORKERS, INC.
767 East Street
Walpole, MA 02081
1-800-343-6948
*Custom-made garden architecture
in cedar: fences, screens, gates,
arbors, covered benches, pergolas,
and gazebos.*

BIBLIOGRAPHY

European Gardens, an Historical Atlas by Virgilio Vercelloni; Rizzoli International, New York, NY; 1990.

Garden Furniture and Ornament by John P. White; Apollo, Poughkeepsie, NY; 1987.

The Garden Gate by Rosemary Verey; Simon & Schuster, New York, NY; 1991.

The Garden Trellis by Roy Strong; Simon & Schuster, New York, NY; 1991.

Gardening Through the Ages by Penelope Hobhouse; Simon & Schuster, New York, NY; 1992.

The House of Boughs, edited by Elizabeth Wilkinson and Marjorie Henderson; Viking, New York, NY; 1985.

Ogden Codman and the Decoration of Houses, edited by Pauline C. Metcalf; The Boston Athenaeum, Boston, MA; 1988.

The Well-Furnished Garden by Michael Balston; Simon & Schuster, New York, NY; 1986.

ACKNOWLEDGMENTS

Garlands of roses to all the individuals and institutions who have helped make this book possible, especially these:

Douglas Askew

Avery Architectural and Fine Arts Library at Columbia University

Tony Badalamente

James R. Bailey

Ernesta and Fred Ballard

Barnsley House

Beinecke Library of Rare Books and Manuscripts at Yale University

Bellingrath Gardens

Michael Berryhill

Birmingham Botanical Garden

Janis Blackschleger

Sally Boasberg

The Boston Athenaeum

Bourton House

Joanna Bristol, Cleveland Botanic Garden

Brooklyn Botanic Garden

Builders' Square

John Burgee

Butchart Gardens

Francis Cabot

Callaway Gardens

Loren Charter

Chelsea Flower Show

Tom Christopher

Cleveland Botanical Garden

Judy Cloninger

Columbus, Ohio, Park of Roses

Lea Davies

Charles De Kay

Denver Botanical Garden

Descanso Gardens

Disneyland

Tim Duval/Plant Specialists

Eubanks-Bohnn Associates

J. Paul Getty Museum

C. Z. Guest

Charles Gulick

Het Loo

Hickey-Robertson

Hope Hendler

Hidcote Manor Garden

Home Depot

Horticultural Society of New York

House Beautiful Magazine: Margaret Kennedy and Sarah McPeck

Houston Photolab: Rhonda Boeske and Douglas McCoy

Robin Davies Hubbard

Huntington Botanical Gardens and Museum

Daniel Janish

Will Johnston

R. Michael Lee

Longue Vue Gardens

Los Angeles State and County Arboretum

Ann Lovejoy

Mr. and Mrs. David B. Martin

Elvin McDonald

Jan Melchior

Lynden and Leigh Miller

Mohonk Mountain House

Mr. and Mrs. Eugene Mosier

National Academy of Design

Nemours

Netherlands Flower-Bulb Institute

New York Botanical Garden

Diane Ofner

Old Westbury Gardens

Oxford Botanic Garden

Hila Paldi

Pennsylvania Horticultural Society

Terry Pierce

Lawrence V. Power

Queens Botanical Garden

Bob Riffle

River Farm

David Robinson

Rosalie Plantation

Rosedown Plantation

Royal Botanical Gardens at Kew

Jerry Sedenko

Josephine Shanks

Sissinghurst Castle

Joe Smiley

Society for the Preservation of New England Antiquities

Stark Cleaning Services: Tino and Richard

Linda Starr

James Steinmeyer

Edwin Toth

John Touchet

Scott Travers

University of British Columbia Botanical Garden

Don Vanderbrook

Edwina Van Gal

Rosemary Verey, Barnsley House

David Walker and Catherine Beason

Benita Warner

Diane Warner

Jan Warner

Jane Warner

Charles D. Webster, Jr.

Herbert C. Wells

John H. Whitworth, Jr.

Tony Williams

Nolan Willis

Michael K. Wilson

Linda and John Yang

Dr. Sun Yat-Sen Classical Chinese Garden

& All the loving members of my family and the able minds and bodies at Macmillan: Pam Hoenig, publisher; Jennie McGregor Bernard, my editor; John Meils for helping keep everything together; and my agent, Carla Glasser.

PHOTO CREDITS

Page 1: Senecio vines augment a lovely sculpture.

Page 2: Ellipses in lattice give way to rose gardens beyond.

Page 3: An 'Excelsa' rose in the Brooklyn Botanic Garden.

Page 6, left: Slat house of Charles D. Webster, Jr., in Long Island, New York.

Page 6, middle: A pavilion is a graceful attachment to any home.

Page 6, right: Detail of the bench at Hetloo in the Netherlands.

Page 11: A rustic gazebo feature at the 1991 Chelsea Flower Show.

Page 12: A union of old stone and metal at the Botanic Gardens in Oxford, England.

Page 13, top: A lattice pavilion at Rosalie in Natchez, Mississippi.

Page 13, bottom: Lacy ironwork crowns the entrances at Hidcote Manor Gardens in Gloucestershire, England.

Page 72: A welcoming niche in the Lattice Garden at Butchart Gardens in Victoria, British Columbia.

Page 73, top: An elegant sweep of roof in Descanso Gardens in La Canada Flintridge, California.

Page 73, bottom: A rusticated lattice pavilion in Sewickley, Pennsylvania.

Page 94: An indoor enclosure takes trompe l'oeil to its ultimate expression.

Page 95, top: Yellow tuberous begonias poke through a window in Sewickly, Pennsylvania.

Page 95, bottom: A summer house at a public garden in Greenwood, South Carolina.

Page 110: A design plan for an arbor covered bench.

Page 111, top: A peak design for a lattice screen.

Page 113, bottom: An arbored-gate design.

Page 140: Brick pillars topped with a log provide excellent support for climbing roses.

Page 141, top: A *Mandevilla* in full bloom.

Page 141, bottom: A *Lapagenia* flower.

Page 176: A mirror ellipse at Hope Hendler's garden in New York, New York.

Page 177, top: An unfinished arbor in the Denver Botanic Garden.

Page 177, bottom: A rustic fence detail from the Mohonk Mountain House near New Paltz, New York.

Page 178: A single clematis flower augments a ball finial.

Page 179: An inviting and mysterious entryway uses bamboo and hints of lattice at the Atlanta Botanic Gardens.

Pages 180–81: The view through the rose pavilion at the Brooklyn Botanic Garden.

Page 182: Seating area at the Butchart Gardens in Victoria, British Columbia.

Pages 184–85: The view from within the lattice pavilion at the Old Westbury Gardens in New York.

Page 187: A quaint pavilion on display at the 1991 Chelsea Flower Show.

Loren Charter: page 79

Tim Duval: pages 76, 77 (left), 77 (right)

Dennis Hall: pages 20 (bottom), 61

Dan Janish: page 78

Hickey-Robertson: pages 48 (top), 109

David Robinson: pages 82, 86, 87, 88, 89 (top)

Allen Rokach: pages 28–29

Joe Smiley: page 80

Computer enhancement by Nolan Willis: pages 98, 104, 120–21, 130, 131, 132–33, 138–39

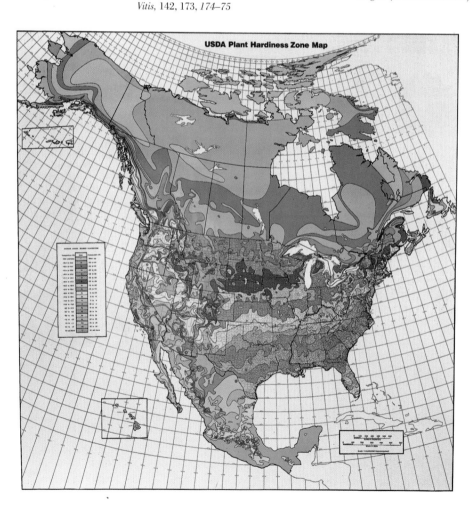